# REFORMING
# DAIRY POLICY

ORGANISATION FOR ECONOMIC CO-OPERATION AND DEVELOPMENT

# ORGANISATION FOR ECONOMIC CO-OPERATION AND DEVELOPMENT

Pursuant to Article 1 of the Convention signed in Paris on 14th December 1960, and which came into force on 30th September 1961, the Organisation for Economic Co-operation and Development (OECD) shall promote policies designed:

- to achieve the highest sustainable economic growth and employment and a rising standard of living in Member countries, while maintaining financial stability, and thus to contribute to the development of the world economy;
- to contribute to sound economic expansion in Member as well as non-member countries in the process of economic development; and
- to contribute to the expansion of world trade on a multilateral, non-discriminatory basis in accordance with international obligations.

The original Member countries of the OECD are Austria, Belgium, Canada, Denmark, France, Germany, Greece, Iceland, Ireland, Italy, Luxembourg, the Netherlands, Norway, Portugal, Spain, Sweden, Switzerland, Turkey, the United Kingdom and the United States. The following countries became Members subsequently through accession at the dates indicated hereafter: Japan (28th April 1964), Finland (28th January 1969), Australia (7th June 1971), New Zealand (29th May 1973), Mexico (18th May 1994), the Czech Republic (21st December 1995) and Hungary (7th May 1996). The Commission of the European Communities takes part in the work of the OECD (Article 13 of the OECD Convention).

Publié en français sous le titre :

RÉFORMER LA POLITIQUE LAITIÈRE

# FOREWORD

In 1987, OECD ministers agreed on the need for concerted reform of agricultural policies, and defined the principles and actions on which such reform should be based. The reform agenda has since been the central focus of the OECD's work on agriculture. Annual monitoring of agricultural policy developments in Member countries and assessment against the Ministerial principles for reform has been one important element of the work. More recently, this has been complemented, particularly in response to guidelines provided by OECD agricultural ministers at their March 1992 meeting, by analyses of linkages between the farm sector and the related upstream and downstream industries in order to gain a better understanding of how government intervention, in particular agricultural policy, affects the agro-food sector as a whole.

This report is one of a number of studies in the Secretariat's work on policies and adjustment in the agro-food sector. It reviews a range of policy approaches and institutional arrangements in the dairy sector, including Canada, Netherlands, New Zealand, United States and United Kingdom, examines their impact on the structure and performance of the industry as a whole, discusses the pressures and options for policy reform and draws a number of general observations pertaining to the reform of agricultural policy. Other related studies have been published as *Technological Change and Structural Adjustment in OECD Agriculture* and *Adjustment in OECD Agriculture: Issues and Policy Responses.*

This report is published on the responsibility of the Secretary General of the OECD as recommended by the Committee for Agriculture in April 1996.

# TABLE OF CONTENTS

## Tables

## Tables annexe

# EXECUTIVE SUMMARY

Across OECD Member countries there is widespread debate on the need for, and direction of, agricultural policy reform. The economic importance of the dairy sector combined with high levels of support have placed dairy policy in the forefront of these discussions in many countries. This paper attempts to examine the impacts of dairy policy on the structure and performance of the dairy industry as a whole. The impetus for this broader agro-food approach comes from the recognition that intra-industry linkages within the food chain can affect the outcomes of agricultural policies and that these policies, generally directed at the farm level, can also influence the structure and perform- ance of upstream and downstream industries

Drawing on the experiences of five OECD Member countries (United States, Canada, New Zealand, United Kingdom, the Netherlands), this study provides an over- view of the kinds of impacts that have been observed across a range of policy approaches and institutional arrangements, with particular reference to downstream processing. Many of the underlying pressures for policy reform (market conditions, international trade agreements, industry structural adjustment, domestic budgetary pressures) are similar across OECD Member countries such that the policy responses of other administrations are of broad interest. In this context, the study also examines the current public policy debate in the countries under review.

The study is not intended to provide a comprehensive assessment of dairy policy for individual countries. Rather a number of observations related to dairy, and agricultural policy reform in general, can be drawn from this study:

- An agro-food approach (assuming impacts beyond the farm gate) to assessing policy impacts is a useful additional perspective given the available evidence that industry linkages along the food chain affect policy outcomes and that agricultural policies influence the structure and performance of related upstream and down- stream industries. Assessing policies against their stated farm level objectives may be an insufficient test if impacts along the food chain are significantly large. The dairy policies examined had and some still have a demonstrable impact on the structure and performance of downstream industries.
- The rationale for existing policies should be carefully evaluated and underlying assumptions questioned, particularly for policy regimes established several decades ago. Structural adjustment, domestic and international market develop- ments, new technologies and other industry changes may combine such that the

7

original justifications for government interventions may no longer apply. The origins of many dairy policies, for example, can be traced back to a time of uncharacteristically low milk prices, severe hardships for dairy farmers and an imbalance of market power.

- Policy objectives should then be reviewed for more consistency against the evolution of the domestic and international contexts. The multiple initial goals which have been set, particularly in the dairy sector, have in time become conflicting with regard to the changes which occurred and have been mentioned in the previous indent. An effective means of addressing the major problem of low farm incomes might be through direct income support which reduces the output effects of price support and can be targeted more easily to poorer dairy farmers. In many cases, sectoral policies may be in direct conflict with broader economic and social policies (*e.g.* fiscal restraint, competition policy, productivity growth, international competitiveness). Government intervention in the dairy sector has generally been in the form of market price support which encourages production and supply controls or intervention buying which are used to offset the resulting market imbalance.

- The Uruguay Round Agreement on Agriculture will have an impact on the dairy industry through some increase in market access for dairy products and reduced export subsidy commitments for butter, skim milk powder and cheese. The impact of reduced export subsidies on downstream processors and exporters could be more significant than initially anticipated. However, little change in the overall level of support and trade flows is anticipated. Nevertheless, countries with no supply control and low support levels are expected to regain market shares at the expense of countries which have to limit their subsidised exports. The discipline on domestic support is unlikely in itself to generate significant change in dairy policy except in the long-run, beyond the implementation period, while tariffs on dairy products have been set so high that little increased trade is likely to occur.

- The pressures for, and benefits from, dairy policy reform will be both domestic and international in nature over the next several years driven by budgetary considerations, market pressures and the impact of the Uruguay Round Agreement. Much of the impetus for change in the near future is likely to come from the industry itself, recognising that it either must make adjustments now or will suffer from fundamental and destabilising changes later as international commitments to reduce levels of protection become more binding and a freer trade regime develops. The interests of the downstream dairy industry are increasingly important in the process of dairy policy reform as governments recognise its significant contributions to employment, value-added manufacturing and trade.

- Fundamental dairy policy reform, including in some cases the removal of supply controls, has been successful. Actual experience in the dairy industry (*e.g.* New Zealand, Australia, Sweden) as well as simulation analysis of the US situation suggest the negative impacts of reform and costs of adjustment may be less significant than commonly anticipated. There are a number of reasons for this including declining dependence on support measures due to past reductions in levels of protection; ongoing industry structural adjustment despite the masking of market signals by policy instruments; overestimating the significance of existing policies for farm household incomes due to relatively low transfer efficiencies and underestimating the ability of the industry to adjust to policy reform.

– One issue briefly touched on in this review of the dairy industry is the potential impact of monopoly/monopsony structures on industry structure and performance. Whether the market power results from government legislation (*e.g.* NZDB) or through aggressive marketing (*e.g.* UK Milk Marque), such structures may affect market competition along the food chain. In addition, where there has been a tradition of anticompetitive arrangements prior to reform, stakeholders may seek ''private'' agreements that continue such arrangements. This has implications for the reform process, in particular the need for complementarity between agricultural policy reform and policies to ensure effective competition.

– Notwithstanding the obvious benefits of substantial reform for the agro-food sector as a whole, the weak justification for much of the continuing intervention and the high cost of support, complete and rapid deregulation may be perceived to be difficult in many countries. The disruption that could result from the abolition of long standing policy regimes if production were to respond more directly to market signals and the demands for compensation by those affected may be seen as having high short-term costs. However, maintaining the existing policy environment and risking the long-run economic health of the sector is equally undesirable. In such cases, one option may be targeted adjustment measures to help offset short-term costs. Still, gradual policy reform can lead to some improvements in the form of programme cost reductions, gains in economic efficiency and greater market orientation.

# REFORMING DAIRY POLICY

## I. Introduction

*Background*

The Committee for Agriculture has placed high priority on gaining a better understanding of how government intervention, in particular agricultural policy, affects the agro-food sector as a whole. The linkages between the farm sector and the related upstream and downstream industries have been identified as the primary focus of the work. Specifically, concerns arise from the recognition that:
- intra-industry linkages within the food chain can affect the eventual outcomes of agricultural policies and policy reforms in terms of economic efficiency, capture of benefits and industry adaptability;
- agricultural policies, which are primarily designed to achieve certain desired objectives at the farm level, can also influence the structure and performance of related upstream and downstream industries.

Examples of some of the policy issues that arise from a broader agro-food perspective were provided in a 1994 OECD consultant's report, *Structural Change in the Dairy Sector of OECD Countries: Recent Trends and Implications for Policies.*[1] In addressing the issue of the economic efficiency of small dairy herds, the report suggested that where the distribution of milk-producing capacity is concentrated in small herds, the industry may be less efficient and that this reduced efficiency carries an economic cost. The report identified the possible emergence of a "two-track" dairy sector, characterised by multiple-job holding farm families at one end and large commercially-orientated specialist dairy farms at the other and questioned the compatibility of these divergent trends with the consumer-driven and technology-led needs of the downstream processing sector for competitively-priced, high-quality products. A third issue raised was whether current policies for the milk-producing segment could continue to be highly regulated alongside the generally much more competitive and market-oriented processing industry. Specifically, the report asked, "Do strong regulation and support policies in dairy farming inhibit or enhance structural change in the processing sector, or are other factors such as the extent to which national processors compete domestically and on international markets more important? Will developments in the processing sector force the pace of moves towards market orientation in dairy farm policy?'' Reviewing the impacts of policy on the agro-food sector as a whole was seen as a useful approach to address these issues.[2]

Support policies and institutional arrangements in the dairy industries of most Member countries will come under review over the period ahead as policy adjustments are made to meet the Uruguay Round obligations. Similarly, domestic priorities such as economic growth, international competitiveness, distributional effects (equity) and budgetary expenditure reductions are likely to bring these interventions under closer scrutiny. In this context of policy review and reform, an assessment of the impact of dairy policy on the structure and performance of the sector as a whole might be timely.

Accordingly, a range of policy approaches and institutional arrangements in OECD Member countries have been examined, including the United States, Canada, New Zealand, the United Kingdom and the Netherlands.[3] The objective of this paper is not to provide a comprehensive assessment of dairy policy for individual countries but rather to provide an overview of some of the impacts of dairy policies with particular reference to the downstream industries. (Only illustrative highlights are presented in the paper; Annex 2 provides a detailed review of the available information on the impacts of dairy policy on sector structure and performance.) In so doing, the paper attempts to draw some general observations about the implications for dairy policy reform and the usefulness of policy assessment from a broader agro-food perspective.

## Importance of the dairy industry

The dairy industry is of considerable importance in all OECD Member countries. At the production level, milk accounts for about 13 per cent of total agricultural output for the OECD as a whole with several EU countries (e.g. Denmark, Germany, the Netherlands, United Kingdom) above 20 per cent.[4] For many of the smaller Member countries including Ireland, Norway, Sweden and Switzerland, milk production represents over one-third of agricultural output. However, milk output has been slightly declining in importance across the OECD area. Nevertheless in Canada and Switzerland, two countries with relatively high levels of support for the dairy industry, milk production has been increasing as a share of total agricultural output.

More than for most agricultural commodities, downstream processing is an integral part of the industry. In most OECD countries, drinking milk represents less than one-third of total processing milk (Table 1), the main exceptions being Japan, Portugal, Spain, the United Kingdom, and the United States. In several countries, including Denmark, France, Ireland, the Netherlands and New Zealand, processed products other than drinking milk account for about 90 per cent of total processing milk. A significant proportion of milk production in OECD Member countries is of higher value-added products such as ice cream and yoghurt.

The total annual value of OECD dairy exports for the 1990-92 period exceeded the value of imports by close to US$5 billion with most of the trade in processed dairy products (Table 2). For processed dairy products, however, imports have been growing at a rate almost double that of exports. The annual growth rate between the 1980-82 and 1990-92 periods was 4 per cent for imports compared with 2.1 per cent for exports. Dairy

Table 1. **Proportion of drinking milk in total processing milk, 1986, 1992**

In percentages

| Country | 1986 | 1992 | Country | 1986 | 1992 |
|---|---|---|---|---|---|
| Australia | 26.9 | 23.7 | Japan[1] | 60.5 | 60.1 |
| Austria | 32.1 | 27.6 | The Netherlands | 5.1 | 4.6 |
| Belgium-Luxembourg | 16.7 | 17.3 | New Zealand | 6.7 | 5.9 |
| Canada | 23.4 | 20.1 | Norway | 24.4 | 11.0 |
| Denmark | 7.2 | 6.9 | Portugal | 57.0[3] | 54.0 |
| Finland | 25.6 | 29.7 | Spain | 72.4 | 63.7[2] |
| France | 10.1 | 8.6 | Sweden | 23.1 | 42.1[1] |
| Germany | 13.8 | 16.4[4] | Switzerland | 20.4 | 20.0 |
| Greece | 28.2 | 29.5[2] | United Kingdom | 44.4 | 50.4 |
| Ireland | 11.9 | 12.0[2] | United States | 38.6 | 37.6 |
| Italy | 30.1 | 18.2 | | | |

1. All fresh products.
2. 1991.
3. 1988.
4. Including Eastern Länder.
*Source:* OECD (1994), *Dairy Sector Indicators*, Paris.


Table 2. **Dairy imports and exports of OECD Member countries**[1]

Current US$ million

| | 1980 82 | 1990-92 | Annual growth rate |
|---|---|---|---|
| **Unprocessed dairy products** [2] | | | |
| Imports | 21 | 41 | +6.8 |
| Exports | 79 | 197 | +9.6 |
| **Processed dairy products** [2] | | | |
| Imports | 1 636 | 2 433 | +4.0 |
| Exports | 5 852 | 7 197 | +2.1 |
| **Total unprocessed products** | | | |
| Imports | 56 787 | 70 683 | +2.2 |
| Exports | 52 167 | 52 951 | +0.1 |
| **Total processed products** | | | |
| Imports | 17 350 | 29 374 | +5.4 |
| Exports | 19 715 | 30 723 | +4.5 |

1. Excludes Turkey, Mexico and Iceland and all intra-EU trade.
2. Unprocessed dairy includes SITC categories fresh milk and cream and whey; all other categories are included in processed dairy products.
*Source:* OECD database.

products are by far the most important agricultural export for the OECD as a whole accounting for almost one-quarter of total processed product exports in 1990-92 although this dominance has diminished over the last decade. With an annual growth rate of 2.1 per cent, exports of dairy products have been growing at less than half of the rate for all processed agricultural products (4.5 per cent).

## II. Government intervention in the dairy industry

Prior to examining the impact of selected dairy policies on the structure and performance of the industry, this section provides some necessary background information. First, a brief overview of the dairy policy regimes to be examined is presented (for a more detailed description see the accompanying Annex 1). The United States, Canada, New Zealand, the Netherlands and the United Kingdom were chosen because they provide a broad range of approaches in terms of the policy instruments used, institutional arrangements employed and overall level of support provided. Also, a number of dairy policy reforms have been introduced or are under discussion in these countries. The second part of this section reviews the rationale for government intervention in the dairy industry. Finally, some quantitative estimates of the level of support to the OECD dairy industry and its costs to taxpayers and consumers are provided.

### Overview of dairy policy in selected OECD countries

In the **United States**, federal dairy price supports and milk marketing orders, import restrictions, export subsidies, domestic and international food aid programs and state milk market regulations all play a role in the production, pricing and marketing of milk and dairy products. The first two instruments, dairy price supports and milk marketing orders, which have the greatest impact on the US dairy industry, were selected for review in this study. Through the Dairy Price Support Programme (DPSP) the government stabilises and supports farm incomes while reducing seasonal instability in milk prices by standing ready to purchase unlimited quantities of specified manufactured dairy products (those are butter, non fat dry milk and cheddar) at established support prices. Import quotas have been used to restrict the inflow of lower-priced foreign products. Federal milk marketing orders are intended to establish orderly marketing conditions and farmer prices by establishing the minimum prices that buyers of milk and milk products must pay and by operating a pooling system for sale proceeds to producers.

The **Canadian** government also provides significant support to the milk and dairy products industry, primarily through legislation which permits the establishment of a highly-administered and complex supply management system. It uses a combination of production and marketing controls (production quotas), import controls (tariff rate quotas) and administered pricing (based on cost of production) to stabilise and support farm income in the dairy sector. The federal government supports the target price through two programs: a direct subsidy to industrial milk producers, and intervention purchasing of surplus butter and skim milk powder. Costs incurred in disposing of surplus dairy products are passed back to producers in the form of levies. No government funding for surplus disposal goes to producers. Fluid milk pricing is under provincial jurisdiction and is based on provincial cost of production formulas, the national industrial milk target price, and end-use. As with the US system, the cost of this support is largely borne by domestic consumers of milk and dairy products rather than by taxpayers.

The *New Zealand* system is significantly different from the policy regimes of other countries considered in this study which are highly protected and focused on the domestic market. New Zealand has an export-oriented, market-based dairy industry which, following fundamental policy reforms in the early and mid-1980s, operates without state subsidies. However, international marketing is still closely controlled. The New Zealand Dairy Board (NZDB) is owned and operated by producer co-operatives and has sole legislated access to NZ dairy products for export. Producer co-operatives, through the Board, exert considerable control over the dairy manufacturing sector since the overwhelming majority of dairy products are exported. Although the dairy processors are independent commercial entities, their product mix is influenced by the NZDB through price purchasing signals and a system of incentives and disincentives.

The dairy industry in the United Kingdom is covered by the *EU Common Agricultural Policy (CAP).* The EU dairy industry still accounts for a significant share of total Community agricultural expenditures (around 13 per cent in 1994). The CAP offers price support for agricultural products through a system of purchasing product surpluses at established floor prices through national intervention boards. In the case of dairy products, only butter and skim milk powder are purchased by intervention boards. Intervention purchases are then disposed of, most importantly through subsidised export sales to non-EU countries. The intervention price effectively provides a floor to the market. A system of variable levies has essentially excluded imports of dairy products, except where special concessions have been negotiated (*e.g.* in the case of New Zealand). In 1984, the EU introduced quotas on milk production in response to market surpluses and the rising cost of sustaining the CAP. The quotas are nationally based and are not transferable across borders. In 1995, even with highly favourable world market conditions, EU dairy sector expenditure amounted to almost 4.3 billion ECU.[5]

While the CAP regime for milk operates throughout the EU, there are some national differences between Member states in the marketing arrangements. For example, in the *United Kingdom,* the Milk Marketing Boards (MMBs), which were abolished in late 1994 (early 1995 in Northern Ireland), operated as monopolies for the purchase of milk under the Milk Marketing Schemes established under the Agricultural Marketing Acts of 1931 and 1933 (the system is more fully described in Annex 1). Prices were set according to end-use and reflected the priority of supply. Receipts from sales were "pooled" and producers were paid a single price adjusted for composition and quality. Under the new arrangements, producers may sell their milk to dairy companies directly, through intermediary organisations managed jointly by producers and dairy companies or through producer groups. Milk Marque, which is the effective successor to MMB in England and Wales, is a co-operative with membership open to any domestic milk producer. It currently accounts for some 50 per cent of UK milk sales.

As with the United Kingdom, dairy policy in the **Netherlands** is governed by the EU Common Agriculture Policy. The Dutch dairy industry has a long standing tradition of operating via co-operatives. Three main co-operatives control over 80 per cent of all milk supplies, giving the industry an oligopoly market structure. Dairy farmers have developed these highly organised co-operatives to perform marketing functions with considerable discriminatory power over individual producers. These co-operatives have the authority to price discriminate between members on the basis of quality standards (in fact, low-quality producers may be expelled from the co-operative).[6] Also, co-operatives can now decide whether or not to accept milk and/or new members according to market opportunities and the returns on investment which can be achieved. To this end, the traditional co-operative policy of free entry of members and acceptance of all milk quantities has been replaced with a more market-oriented policy. The milk quota market is relatively unregulated and is comparable to the transfer conditions in the UK. In the Netherlands, there is no government administrative redistribution of quota as is the case of most other EU countries. With relatively few government restrictions on the transfer of quota, generous tax provisions for the depreciation of quota expenditures and relatively high margins on milk production, quota values in the Netherlands have become among the highest in the EU.

## Role of government intervention

Few, if any, industries are subject to as much government intervention as dairy. Intervention in the dairy industry generally preceded that for most other agricultural commodities and has been the most pervasive. While a few OECD Member countries have removed or significantly reduced the more distortionary forms of intervention in recent years (*e.g.* Australia, New Zealand) and others are reducing to some extent the level of government involvement (*e.g.* Sweden, United Kingdom), most Member countries continue to maintain highly interventionist dairy policy regimes. Why have most governments throughout the OECD become (and remained) so heavily involved in the dairy industry?

### Response to abnormal conditions

Many agricultural policies, introduced in reaction to major economic disruptions, such as depression and war, have tended to become entrenched as features of long-standing agricultural policy. This tendency is particularly evident in the dairy policies of several OECD member countries (especially Northern Europe, North America and Oceania), reflecting the perceived importance of milk in diets. The depression in the 1930s created conditions that favoured intervention, conceived as a response to low and unstable prices in international markets. The effects of the depression led to pressure for greater control and in 1936 the **New Zealand** government assumed monopoly control over all dairy products. The depression also led to the introduction of the US federal programmes and State regulations, with concerns over price stability, orderly marketing, adequate supply and farm income levels cited as motivating factors.

In the **United Kingdom**, the depression led to the establishment of the milk marketing boards to help the industry weather the collapse of world markets, in part influenced by the large scale importation of low priced dairy products from countries such as New Zealand. The second World War also consolidated state intervention to deal with food shortages. An additional problem in the United Kingdom was the dominant market position of a few processing companies in England and Wales, leaving the independent producers in a weak bargaining position (particularly those selling into the industrial milk market). The main functions of the Boards were to provide countervailing power to farmers *vis-à-vis* processors of farm products and to provide more order in unstable markets, thus raising and stabilising farm prices.

In **Canada,** during World War II, federal subsidies were paid to dairy farmers to maintain production levels under a system of wartime price controls. Post-war assistance for industrial milk products, initially intended to be transitional, included programmes to support prices, to export surplus products and to restrict imports. Structures to manage the dairy industry were put in place rather later (in the 1960s and 1970s) than in other advanced industrial countries. This was partly driven by the need to negotiate a national policy between the federal government and the provinces, but was also seen as a response to changing world market conditions in part caused by government interventions in the dairy sector in other countries.

The **EU** dairy policy, with its import levies, intervention buying and export subsidies, was established in 1962 with the adoption of the CAP.[7] CAP goals included a fair return to farmers, stable markets, assurance of supplies, reasonable consumer prices, and the introduction of policies designed to increase yield and labour productivity. Because the EU (then referred to as the European Community) was a net importer at the time, the creation and use of export subsidies to make its dairy products competitive on world markets was not costly. However, as it became a net exporter (in the mid 1970s), CAP costs increased dramatically. This eventually led to the implementation of the quota system in 1984.

*Multiple and conflicting objectives*

Dairy policies have been saddled with multiple objectives which have become increasingly conflicting over time. For example, small dairy operations have commonly been seen as the typical family farm; the survival of which has often been an implicit or explicit political priority. In some regions, dairy production is still regarded as a basic family farming activity to be protected for its social implications. Also, in areas not suitable for arable crops, dairy production has often been promoted as a good alternative for local development, especially in mild-climate, disadvantaged areas. At the same time, the desire for cost-reducing and production enhancing productivity gains fuelled substantial government investment in dairy research and technology transfers which, in turn, encouraged farm expansion and increased output. Thus, intensive dairy operations have become much more economic than extensive pasture-based operations. Social, economic, regional and, more recently, environmental objectives have all influenced the evolution of dairy policy in Member countries. The following objectives, common to many OECD countries, are typical of the broad mandate associated with dairy policy:

- farm income stabilisation;
- a fair return to producers;
- protection of the family farm;
- protection of regional production capability;
- provision of an adequate supply of quality products at reasonable prices to consumers;
- reduced government financial support;
- enhance market orientation and industry adaptability.

As a 1983 OECD review of dairy policy observed, "The current study has high-lighted the awesome array of roles which the dairy sector is required to play in Member countries. It is not sufficient that the sector should provide a regular, assured and adequate supply of essential but perishable milk and milk-based food stuffs. In almost all countries, it is expected to fulfil wider social and even strategic objectives, including the prevention of urban drift and rural depopulation, the maintenance of rural employment opportunities, and certain other regional and environmental considerations".[8]

*Creation of vested interests*

Taxpayers and consumers would clearly benefit from changes to the present dairy policies and institutional arrangements. Many producers and downstream industries could also benefit from policy reform as evidenced in Sections III and IV. However, reforms are often perceived to be difficult to implement. One reason is that dismantling elaborate and complex dairy policy regimes inevitably involves economic and social costs and it is not always evident how to balance the greater public benefit against the costs imposed on particular groups such as smaller farmers and disadvantaged regions. Even where dairy farmers are not disadvantaged relative to other producers or by economy-wide standards, the capitalisation of high average levels of support and quota arrangements can lead to significant production rents which provide strong incentives for producers to resist change. Different approaches used to address problems of over-supply (*e.g.* enhance demand, mandatory quotas, reduce prices, set-aside schemes, retirement programmes) have met with varying levels of success. Many schemes succeed in taking some farmers and cows out of dairying and keep production below what it otherwise would have been but do not halt the long-term upward trend in output.

Another reason reforms are perceived to be difficult to implement is the relative importance of the dairy industry to the agriculture sector as a whole. Today, in most OECD Member countries, the dairy industry remains a major component of the agriculture sector and, therefore, the sector as a whole is more sensitive to changes in dairy support policies. However, part of this development is due to past agricultural policies that encouraged dairying. Table 3 presents information on the specialisation and fre-quency (or incidence) of dairy operations for 17 OECD countries which confirms the significant role of the dairy industry. A high frequency indicates a large proportion of producers are involved in dairying (*e.g.* more than 35 per cent of producers in Belgium,

Table 3.  **Specialisation and frequency of dairying**

| Frenquency | Specialisation | | | |
| --- | --- | --- | --- | --- |
| | < 30% of dairy herds on specialist dairy farms | 30-50% of dairy herds on specialist dairy farms | 50-70% of dairy herds on specialist dairy farms | > 70% of dairy herds on specialist dairy farms |
| Dairy herds on < 25% of farms | Greece Portugal | Spain Italy | United States Japan | United Kingdom Finland Canada |
| Dairy herds on 25-35% of farms | | | Denmark France | Ireland Norway Sweden |
| Dairy herds on > 35% of farms | | Belgium | Germany | Netherlands |

*Note:*   All information relates to 1987, except for Finland (1990), Japan (1990), Canada (1991), Norway (1992) and Sweden (1990). Farm type definitions are not strictly comparable across OECD countries. For EC countries, farm type definitions are based on the EC typology, which classifies farms according to the break-down of their gross margin over different activities. Japan, Norway, Sweden and US apply national definitions.

*Source:*   OECD (1995), *Structural Change in the Dairy Sector of OECD Countries: Recent Trends and Implications for Policies*, Paris. Information for Canada supplied separately by the Ministry of Agriculture and Agro-Food.

Germany, Netherlands). A high degree of specialisation implies the agricultural income of those producers is more dependent on the dairy enterprise (*e.g.* more than 70 per cent of dairy herds on specialist farms in the United Kingdom, Finland, Ireland, Norway, Sweden, Netherlands). One would expect to find dairy pressure groups and producer organisations more active and powerful in those countries to the right and to the lower part of the table.

Considerable literature exists on the political economy or the decision making process as it relates to the dairy industry.[9] The general thesis of this work is that the complexity of issues relating to the dairy sector discourages intervention from those outside the sector. As noted in one US study, "Throughout the 1970s, when presidents were struggling to control inflation and were willing to take politically risky initiatives on behalf of pro-competitive deregulation to that end, they were constantly on the defensive concerning milk price supports. From their perspective, the issue was not whether to put an end to government interventions, it was whether to resist (and, if so, how hard) the efforts of an aggressive Congress urged on by a very rich and very active dairy lobby, to drive price supports up".[10]

## Costs of intervention

### Support level

**Producer subsidy equivalents** (PSE) and **consumer subsidy equivalents** (CSE) provide estimates of the level of support to agricultural production. The PSE is an

Table 4.  **Milk PSE and CSE for OECD as a whole**

|  | 1986-88 | 1990-92 | 1993 | 1994ᶜ |
|---|---|---|---|---|
| Milk PSE (US$ mn) | 42 219 | 55 349 | 49 308 | 49 756 |
| % of total PSE | 29 | 32 | 30 | 28 |
| Milk CSE (US$ mn) | –34 141 | –41 234 | –36 838 | –37 903 |
| % of total CSE | 29 | 32 | 30 | 30 |

e:    estimate.
*Source:*    OECD Secretariat.

indicator of the value of monetary transfers to agricultural producers resulting from agricultural policies, in a given year. Both transfers from consumers of agricultural products (through domestic market prices) and transfers from taxpayers (through budgetary or tax expenditure) are included. The CSE is and indicator of the value of monetary transfers to consumers resulting from agricultural policies in a given year. It comprises both transfers to (or more commonly from) domestic consumers due to market price support policies, and transfers from taxpayers to consumers of agricultural products. CSEs differ from PSEs in that they exclude direct payments and other budgetary expenditures which raise the effective price received by producers but do not raise the price paid by consumers. When negative, the CSE can be viewed as an implicit tax on consumers imposed by agricultural policies.

As shown in Table 4, the 1994 milk PSE is estimated at US$49.8 billion for the OECD area as a whole, down from 1992 but still 8 per cent above the 1986-88 level (a period including the time of the 1987 Ministerial Communiqué on agricultural policy reform calling for increased market orientation and reduced levels of support). The milk CSE for 1994 is estimated at US$38 billion. The milk PSE and CSE account for the largest proportion of total support, representing about 30 per cent of the total net PSE and CSE.

PSEs and CSEs are also calculated as a percentage of the value of production (or consumption) valued at domestic producer prices. The *percentage PSE/CSE* measures provide an indication of the relative level of support across OECD Member countries. The 1994 percentage PSE and CSE for milk were 62 and 53 per cent, respectively, for the OECD as a whole (Table 5). In most Member countries, the dairy industry receives by far the highest levels of support as measured by percentage PSEs and CSEs, exceeding 60-70 per cent of the value of production in many cases. For Australia, Canada and the United States, for example, milk PSEs are 2-3 times higher than the average for all commodities (although still relatively low in Australia compared with other countries). New-Zealand, which has undergone comprehensive policy reform, is the one exception with very low levels of support for most commodities including dairy.

Table 5. **Percentage PSE and CSE, by country, 1994**e

| | Percentage PSE | | Percentage CSE | |
| --- | --- | --- | --- | --- |
| | Milk | All PSE Commodities | Milk | All CSE Commodities |
| Australia | 31 | 10 | −31 | −7 |
| Austria | 71 | 61 | −65 | −53 |
| Canada | 67 | 26 | −56 | −19 |
| EU | 61 | 49 | −51 | −38 |
| Finland | 71 | 69 | −70 | −65 |
| Iceland | 83 | 72 | −62 | −40 |
| Japan | 90 | 74 | −74 | −50 |
| New Zealand | 2 | 3 | 0 | −5 |
| Norway | 78 | 74 | −64 | −57 |
| Sweden | 66 | 52 | −58 | −43 |
| Switzerland | 83 | 81 | −45 | −59 |
| Turkey | 49 | 34 | −37 | −24 |
| United States | 52 | 20 | −46 | −10 |
| OECD average | 61 | 42 | −52 | −33 |

e:   estimate.
*Source:*   OECD Secretariat.

## Other economic costs

Moreover, agricultural support policies have adverse affects that go beyond their impact on public and consumer expenditure. A recent OECD report estimated that the average 1986-88 levels of agriculture support could have cost OECD countries (Australia, Canada, EU, Japan, New Zealand, United States) as a whole almost 1 per cent in terms of lower real household income ($72 billion in 1988 prices and exchange rates).[11] This cost seems even more disproportionate when viewed in the context of the small share of agro-food in most economies; about 6 per cent of total OECD GDP. These costs arise because agricultural assistance:

- wastes resources by over-expanding output in the agro-food sector at the expense of other industries;
- tends to push up land rents, which then get capitalised into higher land prices;
- increases food prices to OECD consumers and taxes to the public;
- tends to widen the dispersion of wedges between domestic and world prices for many agro-food items; and worsens the terms of trade for many food-exporting countries;
- incurs high costs of administration, implementation and control.

***Total welfare losses*** associated with support to the dairy industry are difficult to measure but some attempts have been made. In Canada, for example, rough estimates suggest that, in addition to the estimated C$ 2 billion CSE for dairy, there were consumer welfare losses of C$ 450 million in foregone demand.[12] Additional welfare losses to society were identified in the form of inefficiencies at the farm and processing level resulting from smaller scale production units, lower capacity plant utilisation and barriers to rationalisation which lead to a distribution of production and processing activities that does not fully reflect regional comparative advantages. Processors, distributors and retailers were also said to exert some degree of market power and, therefore, were able to extract rents from consumers. Moreover, it was pointed out that importers who hold dairy product import quotas capture the difference between domestic and world market prices as pure profit.

Considerably more work is available on the total welfare impacts of dairy policy in the United States. On average over 1980-90, Kaiser found that *producer surplus* was US$1 billion per year (25 per cent) higher due to the Dairy Price Support Programme (DPSP).[13] This estimate is comparable to the estimated long run impact calculated by Helmberger and Chen, who found that the DPSP increased producer surplus by US$763 million annually based on 1990 conditions.[14] Support as measured by PSE estimates has since been reduced.

Estimates of the wholesale cheese and butter gross margins net of raw milk costs with and without the DPSP can be calculated based on data from the Kaiser study. Results indicate that cheese manufacturers were better off without the DPSP since the programme increases their raw milk cost more than it increases the wholesale cheese price. Over the 1980-90 period, simulated wholesale cheese margins averaged US$1.56/lb under the DPSP compared to US$3.58/lb without the programme. In contrast, butter manufacturers were found to be better off with the DPSP since the increase in the wholesale butter price due to the DPSP more than outweighs the increase in raw milk costs. Over this period, simulated wholesale butter margins averaged $6.82/lb with the DPSP compared to US$2.58/lb without the programme. It is more difficult to calculate fluid milk and frozen product margins based on Kaiser's study because the author used price indices for these products. However, since Kaiser's results indicated much larger wholesale price increases under the DPSP for butter, fluid milk, and frozen products than cheese, it seems likely that fluid milk and frozen product processors are beneficiaries of the DPSP. Dairy co-operatives likely benefit more from the DPSP than proprietary processors because co-operatives are the primary ''balancers'' of the market and consequently are the main seller of dairy products to the government. Proprietary processors, on the other hand, typically do not buy more milk than is needed to meet commercial and inventory demand.

Helmberger and Chen estimated rather small losses in *consumer welfare* due to the DPSP. Regarding fluid milk consumer surplus, the study found that the DPSP resulted in an annual loss of US$220 million based on 1990 conditions. The loss in manufacturing consumer surplus was estimated to be US$449 million per year based on conditions prevailing in 1990. Kaiser did not calculate consumer surplus measures in his study, however, he did conclude that consumers would likely be better off without the DPSP since wholesale prices for all dairy products were substantially lower (this assumes that the impact of the DPSP on wholesale prices is the same as its impact on retail prices). Kaiser did not, however, consider the fact that consumers benefit from increased price stability due to the DPSP; albeit at a cost to consumers.

*Taxpayers* would be better off without the DPSP since this program has involved fairly high governmental outlays in the past. Based on 1980s data, Tauer and Kaiser estimated that the net monetary costs of removing a hundred pounds of milk from the market under the DPSP was 0.85 times the farm support price.[15] The parameter, 0.85, accounts for all monetary costs associated with DPSP minus a computed value for foreign and domestic donations, which were valued at 50 per cent of the purchase prices for the products. Using Tauer and Kaiser's results, the average net monetary cost of the DPSP from 1980-90 was US$1.1 billion per year. However, at the same time, it should be noted that these costs have been steadily decreasing in both nominal and real terms since 1988 due to lower support prices and lower purchases by the CCC.

Helmberger and Chen estimated the following *national welfare impacts* of milk marketing orders. Regarding producer welfare, it was estimated that the short-run impact of eliminating marketing orders would be an US$860 million loss in producer surplus annually based on 1990 conditions. The long-run impact on producer surplus was about one-half of this, US$444 million per year. With respect to fluid milk, the authors estimated that milk marketing orders decreased consumer surplus by US$1.2 billion (short-run) and US$1 billion (long-run) per year based on 1990 conditions. In terms of manufacturing milk consumer welfare, the study found an increase in consumer surplus of US$354 million (short-run) and US$648 million (long-run) per year based on 1990 conditions.

An interregional study by Chavas, Cox, and Jesse found that milk marketing orders increased national producer surplus by US$519 million per year, or 2 per cent of the competitive equilibrium solution.[16] Milk marketing orders were estimated to have reduced fluid and manufactured milk consumer surplus by US$243 million per year, or 0.3 per cent of the competitive solution. The regional losers due to milk marketing orders would be the more efficient dairy regions of California, Wisconsin, and the Upper Midwest while producers in other regions of the United States would experience gains in producer surplus due to milk marketing orders. There are no net monetary government costs to tax payers of milk marketing orders. Rather, the administrative costs of milk marketing orders is paid primarily by regulated milk handlers by assessments on the amount they handle.

A more recent report by ABARE[17] estimated the cost to the US economy from resource misallocation arising from support for milk production using a comparative static model. Starting from a model-generated assumption that a unilateral removal of all agricultural support in the US would increase world prices for dairy products by 23.5 per cent, the report estimated, for the period 1991-93, dead-weight losses at US$1 billion for production and US$0.2 billion for consumption. The aggregate loss to the US economy from US dairy policy is therefore US$1.2 billion.

## Ongoing public debate

Despite the economic importance and political sensitivity of the dairy industry, there have been significant dairy policy developments in recent years. A number of countries have undertaken reform programmes impinging on the dairy industry. The most notable examples are the dismantling of all support measures to the dairy industry in New Zealand, reductions to already low support levels for dairy producers in Australia, the abolition of the UK milk marketing boards and the limited moves made in Sweden before accession to the European Union toward market orientation and deregulation (*e.g.* elimination of quotas, the two-price system and export subsidies). The United States introduced two voluntary supply management programmes in the 1980s, the Milk Diversion Programme and the Dairy Termination Programme, attempted to bring milk supplies into balance with demand and exert upward pressure on milk prices but had only short-term effects. At the same time, minimum support prices have been frozen for the last few years.

Public debate over dairy policy continues, fuelled by such issues as low transfer efficiencies and capture of programme benefits, high costs to consumers and taxpayers, conflicting interests between various levels of the food chain, regional inequities and concerns over increasing international competition. There is a wide range of policy approaches and types of institutional arrangements operating within the OECD dairy industry. Many of these interventions have been identified as having significant influences on the structure and performance of downstream industries. For example:

- In the *United States,* the Federal milk marketing order system has been the subject of much debate with concerns about price discrimination between fluid and industrial milk, over-production, regional imbalances between milk production and processing, and reduced milk prices for non-regulated producers.
- In *Canada,* institutional rigidities in the dairy supply management scheme which result in restrictions on the transferability of quotas, inter-provincial trade barriers and high prices for raw milk used in processing have been seen as at least partially responsible for a lack of market responsiveness and competitiveness-enhancing structural adjustment.
- In *Japan,* liquid and manufacturing milk prices are pooled regionally resulting in significant differences in ''average'' farm-level prices across prefectures while dairy product mix is influenced by support measures (*e.g.* deficiency payments, intervention buying and monopoly control over imports) which are restricted to certain designated products.
- In the *EU,* notwithstanding a common regime for farm level support, there are different downstream arrangements in place. The *UK* Milk Marketing Boards, which were monopsonistic buyers from producers and monopolist sellers in the wholesale milk market, were an exception and are now dismantled. This is expected to facilitate a number of downstream structural adjustments leading to efficiency gains in the form of increased innovation and value-added, larger and more diversified dairies and higher plant utilisation rates.
- In *Sweden,* before the accession to the European Union, the considerable adjustment required by downstream processors was a major obstacle to policy reform in the dairy industry because the old price equalisation scheme had led many processors to specialise in the production of skim milk powder, butter or cheese since the levy on liquid milk was redistributed to other products.
- In *New Zealand,* the producer-controlled Dairy Board is independent of the government and has a control power over all exports,[18] setting export prices and

quantities for each dairy product, purchasing all export requirements from the co-operative dairy companies and influencing the product mix of manufacturers by regulating price differentials between milk products.

## III. Dairy policy impacts on industry structure and performance

This section provides an indication of some of the key impacts of dairy policies and institutional arrangements in the United States, Canada, New Zealand, the United Kingdom and the Netherlands on the structure and performance of the dairy industry as a whole based on available research. An objective is to highlight some of the implications for the downstream dairy processing industry. A more extensive discussion of policy impacts, upon which this section is based, is presented in Annex 2.

### *Impacts on structure*

*Resource allocation*

- In the United States, the DPSP has resulted in excess milk production of 6-8 per cent since the 1980s. Excess production of manufactured dairy products for the 1990-93 period were significantly higher based on CCC purchases (42 per cent of commercial demand for non-fat dry milk, 41 per cent of commercial demand for butter).
- In the United Kingdom and the Netherlands, membership in the EU and access to milk support prices under the EU Common Agriculture Policy (CAP) led to production increases. With the expansion of production, an increasing share of output went into downstream processing. Demand growth did not keep pace with the expansion in processed products with intervention buying "disposing" of the surplus.
- In the Netherlands, the number of small dairy farms continues to decline despite high levels of support, as it is often more attractive to lease or sell quota than to continue production. Young entrants find it increasingly difficult to find sufficient capital to finance inter-generational transfers or to acquire additional quota for farm expansion.

*Supply controls*

- Quotas were introduced in 1984 under the CAP in response to growing intervention stocks and have since been cut back. The impact on the UK and Dutch milk processing industry has been significant, particularly for the intervention products of butter and skim milk powder, as the introduction of quotas has reduced supplies and created excess processing capacity.
- With controls on production, Dutch co-operatives competed aggressively for available milk supplies bidding up the price of raw milk and tried to import milk

in an attempt to avoid plant closures while private processing firms moved more quickly to rationalise capacity.
- The Canadian dairy supply management system uses quotas to limit surplus production but dairy programme benefits (*e.g.* high and stable incomes, high rates of return, high profitability) have been capitalised into quota values (and other fixed asset values). The supply management policies tend to increase production rents rather than protect smaller, higher cost operations or employment opportunities.

*Regional distribution*

- US milk marketing orders impact on the regional distribution of dairy production and processing. A shift in relative milk prices across regions under the 1985 Farm Bill led to significant growth in milk production in some areas. California manufacturers have a higher negotiated processing margins which puts other manufacturers at a competitive disadvantage and has created regional tensions.
- The Canadian supply management system affects regional distribution of production and processing by regulating provincial market shares which have not changed significantly since introduction of the programme. It is difficult for milk processors to adjust to changing market demands as the supply management system does not easily allow for the reallocation of quota rights that would be necessary to develop new products or new markets.
- The operation of quotas within the EU has had the effect of locking-in the location of milk production by country that existed in 1984. Although provisions exist in the EU regulations for quotas to be tradable within member States, in practice, there is little private trading of quota except in the UK and the Netherlands, with quota movements mainly resulting from administrative transfers. Nevertheless, structural adjustments continued at a rapid pace in the EU (for example, since the implementation of quotas, the number of dairy farms in France decreased from 400 000 to 167 000 in 1995, while the average delivery per farm increased from 67 000 to 147 000 litres per year).

*Scale of activity*

- High levels of support in Canada have helped provide assistance to small family farms although the decline in the number of dairy farms has generally been greater than for other less-protected sectors of agriculture over the last several decades. The limited availability of quota combined with numerous quota restrictions on individual producers have inhibited farm size growth and the maximisation of economies of size. Relatively high production costs mean Canadian producers cannot compete effectively in international markets and the domestic market is growing at a significantly slower rate than the US and world dairy markets.

- In the United Kingdom and the Netherlands production quota restrictions limit the availability of supplies to processors. Since it is unlikely that it would be profitable to import large quantities of milk for processing from other countries, quotas also have an effect of limiting the scale of manufacturing activities. In spite of this quota constraint, the level of processing activities increased within the EU, due to marketing considerations and related developments in consumers' habits.
- The number of Dutch processing firms operating has declined by 60 per cent over the 10 years since the introduction of quotas. Some of the large multinationals relocated processing activities to areas where raw milk prices were lower.

*Market power*

- The NZDB controls exports but does not have any direct control of production and cannot capture true monopoly profits. The Board does have exclusive access to dairy products for export and, since the majority of production is exported, this producer-controlled Board exerts a strong influence on downstream processing. The Board can increase farmer returns through price discrimination by ensuring high-priced markets are not flooded and that markets are developed in an orderly manner.
- With the demise of the UK Milk Marketing Boards, market power has, to a large extent, been maintained by producers through the establishment of the voluntary producer-owned co-operatives. The successor body to the Milk Marketing Board for England and Wales, Milk Marque, currently accounts for some 50 per cent of milk delivered to processors in the UK.

**Impacts on performance**

*Product prices*

- Various simulation studies suggest US farm milk prices have been 15-23 per cent higher under the DPSP. Prices at the wholesale level were also raised significantly, with butter prices (the most supported product) 40 per cent higher with the DPSP than without. However, the DPSP impact on wholesale prices is likely less today given declining purchase prices for dairy products.
- The Canada-US price differential increased from virtually nil in the early 1980s to an exchange rate adjusted differential of C$ 6.00/hl by mid-1989. This change was due to a steady decline in US support prices while Canada continued to increase the base price for industrial milk. For some products, such as yoghurt and ice cream, Canadian processors pay up to 50 per cent more for industrial milk.
- The UK Milk Marketing Boards operated a regulated pricing system whereby, through a process of negotiation, and where necessary independent arbitration, the Joint Committee set prices based on the end-use of milk. This system contributed to relatively low producer milk prices in the UK by obscuring market forces and removing the incentive of processors to maximise the value of milk in their

products. Further, in setting prices, the system took account of market conditions and average processing costs, including the costs of excess capacity, a factor exacerbated by the introduction of, and subsequent cuts in, milk quota.
- The NZDB has the potential to act as a price discriminating firm on international markets and thus capture any benefits from price differences which may exist across markets. However, the level of competition for bulk dairy products in international dairy products is such that there are few opportunities for effective price discrimination beyond simple control of product mix (*e.g.* reducing the production of products with inelastic demand).


*Economic efficiency*

- The DPSP has reduced interregional competition in US manufactured dairy products by providing an outlet for surplus production. Government purchases have prevented dairy products from low cost areas from displacing products in other higher cost regional markets. DPSP purchases have also protected processors whose plant capacity is not well aligned with the commercial markets (*e.g.* butter rather than cheese processing).
- The supply management system has contributed to a lack of competitiveness in the Canadian dairy industry. Canadian milk production costs are above those in the US, more than double those of Ireland and more than three times those of New Zealand. Canadian dairy processing plants have lower volume throughputs with the US processing 9 times as much milk from 6 times as many plants.
- It has been suggested that the pooling of returns under the NZDB may lead to inefficiencies. Where prices are pooled and the actual returns to additional production are masked, there may be over-production and maximum benefits would not be captured from the market.
- The payment of a single price to UK dairy producers for milk across each Board region denied the principles of specialisation in production according to competitive advantage which should be reflected in spatial and temporal price differences. The regulated pricing system reduced the incentive for processors to become more efficient since "inefficiency" was passed back to the dairy farmers in the form of lower manufacturing milk prices.
- In the Netherlands, it has been the most intensive dairy operations with the highest margins that have been able to acquire additional quota, presumably leading to some gains in overall sector efficiency although many smaller farms wishing to expand have been unable to bid successfully for available quota. This structural adjustment is somewhat at odds with Dutch agri-environmental policy which encourages more extensive farming practices.


*Industry adaptability*

- In the United States, milk marketing orders have contributed to excess fat production relative to commercial needs as milk has been priced based on volume and fat content despite increasing demand for low-fat products. For a long time, no premiums were paid for other nutritional components such as protein even though protein content increases manufactured product (*e.g.* cheese) yields.

– While Canada's supply management system allows for the movement of quota among provinces, in theory very little reallocation of existing quota has occurred in practice. The result is an allocation that doesn't fully reflect provincial comparative advantage nor fully respond to changes in provincial population patterns and market opportunities.

– Large producer-controlled marketing boards like the NZDB may lack innovation. There have been cases cited which suggest that some opportunities have not been actively pursued. This concern has to some extent been addressed by the current policy of allowing other firms to export certain approved products. Besides, some suggests that the innovative potential of large co-operatives is no less than the one of comparably-sized multinational firms.

– Before the phasing out of the MMB, the combination in the UK of the CAP arrangements and operation of the UK milk marketing system reduced the incentives for efficient processing and enabled the survival of manufacturers whose basic aim was to produce bulk products and shielded those manufacturers from price competition through the formula pricing system. The institutional environment has not favoured innovative activity by UK firms with much of the higher value-added processing within the country carried on by foreign firms.

– The dairy processing sector in the EU is generally innovative, with solid technological know-how and on-going research activities. Dutch dairy co-operatives, for example, have become much more market-oriented in an attempt to gain and maintain market share by restricting membership, tighter quality controls on producers and greater investment in product and market development. The changing role of these co-operatives from producer organisations to marketing firms raises concerns about the conflicting interests of producer members and those of its investors.

## IV. Pressures for reform and policy options

There is considerable public debate about the need and appropriate directions for dairy policy reforms. In this section, some of the pressures for policy reform and some of the reforms under consideration or underway in the countries under review are discussed. A brief review of dairy and the Uruguay Round Agreement is presented first, followed by some of the domestic pressures for reform.

The ***Uruguay Round Agreement*** on Agriculture introduces a new period of policy adjustment which will eventually lead to reduced levels of support.[19] The discipline on domestic support is unlikely in itself to generate any change in dairy policy except in the long-term, beyond the implementation period. This is because of the aggregate nature of the commitments. Countries can concentrate their reduction efforts in other products and generally have. In the EU, because the aggregate measure of support (AMS) covers only butter and skim milk powder, the commodity AMS has fallen significantly since the production of these two commodities has fallen, even though overall milk production has not. The main impact of the UR Agreement on the dairy industry over the implementation period will be from reductions in export subsidies and some increases in market access for imports through the current and minimum access provisions.

An important feature of the Agreement was the conversion of all non-tariff barriers affecting agricultural products into tariff equivalents (with agreement not to introduce new non-tariff measures in the future) and reduction commitments of 36 per cent (calculated on a simple unweighted average basis) with a minimum rate of reduction of 15 per cent for each tariff line. As implementation of the Agreement is to be phased-in over a 6 year period and further lags in adjustment of production, consumption and trade would likely occur, the full effects are not expected to be felt until well into the next decade. Moreover, the initial tariffs have been set at such high levels for the basic dairy products in most cases that, even by the end of the implementation period, trade is unlikely to flow over them. A significant benefit of the tariff equivalents is their transparency.

Table 6 provides a comparison of the *ad valorem* equivalents (AVE) for the base rate tariffs (1986-88) submitted under the UR Agreement with those based on price-gap estimates for skim milk powder and butter for several OECD Member countries. With the exception of Australia, the base rate AVE is significantly above the price-gap based AVE. Notwithstanding the rather high tariff levels, it is expected that over time further negotiations could contribute further to reducing production as well as trade distortion in dairy

Table 6. **Comparison of the *ad valorem* equivalents of the base tariff and the unit market price support 1986-88**

Per cent

|  | Skim milk powder | | Butter | |
|---|---|---|---|---|
|  | Base rate AVE[1] | MPS AVE[2] | Base rate AVE[1] | MPS AVE[2] |
| United States | 166 | 60 | 138 | 134 |
| EU-12 | 146 | 90 | 254 | 199 |
| Canada | 175 | 129 | 320 | 260 |
| Japan | 311 | 227 | 657 | 507 |
| Australia | 3 | 22 | 6 | 27 |
| Switzerland | 99 | 51 | 953 | 823 |

1. Base rate AVE refers to the *ad valorem* equivalent of the base rate used in the GATT country schedules and which apply from the implementation of the Agreement on Agriculture. Where the tariff is expressed as an *ad valorem* rate, it is simply reproduced here. Where the base rate is a specific duty or a combination of an *ad valorem* and a specific rate, the *ad valorem* equivalent has been calculated using as the denominator the external reference price reported in the context of the International Dairy Agreement.
2. MPS AVE refers to the unit market price support expressed as an *ad valorem* equivalent tariff where the denominator is the same external reference price. Domestic prices are wholesale or support prices. Where appropriate and feasible, data used in the calculation of the unit market price support has been established on a comparable basis to data on domestic wholesale prices and world prices used in the tariff calculations.
*Source:* OECD (1995) *The Uruguay Round: A Preliminary Evaluation of the Impacts of the Agreement on Agriculture in the OECD Countries*, Paris.

markets and to improving the allocation of resources in the dairy industry. The Agreement provides for a resumption of negotiations for agriculture by the year 2000 to enable further progress towards the achievement of the agreed long-term objective of substantial progressive reductions in support and protection.

In response to the new GATT commitments on reduced export subsidies, EU dairy exports will have to be cut back by 2.5 million tonnes in milk equivalents over the next six years unless *a)* there is a shift in production from cheese to butter and SMP, *b)* new markets for exports without refunds are developed or *c)* there is growth in internal markets.[20] Commitments on market access imply an additional 1.3 million tonnes of imported milk, mainly in the form of cheese. Restrictions on the subsidised volumes and expenditures apply individually to four product groups: cheese, butter, SMP and other dairy products. As butter and SMP subsidised exports have fallen since the 1986-90 base period, they could increase over the next six years (200 000 tonnes for butter; 100 000 tonnes for SMP). Conversely, in the case of cheese, subsidised exports are well above the base period and must decline by about 18 per cent (130 000 tonnes) from the 1994 level. Finding markets for exports without refunds may be difficult given current EU support levels, even at the relatively high current world price levels. An increase in internal market disposal of 0.5 per cent would reduce the need for exports by 5 per cent, however, growth in internal consumption has been weak and internal supplies will increase under minimum access commitments and East Europe-agreements.

The United States opted to use the flexibility provisions of the UR Agreement to begin phasing down its export subsidies from the average of actual subsidised exports in 1991 and 1992 for both butter and SMP, although the value of subsidies must still be reduced by 36 per cent, and volumes by 21 per cent from the 1986-90 base period averages. Permitted subsidised exports by the year 2000 for butter, SMP and cheese will decline by about 22 000, 40 000 and 800 tonnes, respectively. Relative to total US production of 600 000 tonnes of butter, 400 000 tonnes of SMP and almost 3 million tonnes of cheese, the eventual reductions in subsidised exports will be.[18] Minimum access commitments imply the quota for butter will increase from 320 to 7 000 tonnes by the year 2000. SMP access quota is to be increased from 820 to 5 500 tonnes and cheese from 111 000 to 140 000 tonnes. This is a significant increase in US market access although small relative to world trade (*e.g.* world dairy trade in 1993: 824 000 tonnes of butter, 1 030 000 tonnes of SMP, 974 000 tonnes of cheese).

Recent information on the implementation of UR Agreement may exert greater pressures on the processed food products than have been generally recognised.[21] Due to the growth in export markets for EU processed food (non-Annex II) products since the 1986-90 base period, the GATT export subsidy commitments may pose a serious threat to exports of processed food products in the 1995/96 marketing year. The EU did not make any commitments to limit the volume of non-Annex II products, however, because non-Annex II products such as sugar and dairy are eligible for export refunds (to compensate food processing firms for the high cost of agricultural raw materials under the CAP) the EU does have a commitment on budgetary expenditures on these subsidies. The maximum subsidy expenditure is fixed at 646.1 million ECU (declining to 366.4 million ECU by 2000/2001) compared with 699.6 million ECU in 1992 and 743.5 million ECU in 1993.

Initially, the anticipated reductions in price support associated with CAP reform were expected to lead to reductions in refunds and, in fact, export subsidies for processed cereals have been reduced significantly. However, EU price levels for dairy (and sugar) products have not been affected. This, combined with the growth in processed exports since the UR reference figures were established, means the EU may be in danger of exceeding its GATT commitments for processed food products. The drop in EU export refunds has already been linked to a decline in French dairy products exports which fell by 20 per cent (FF 500 million) over the two months July and August 1995.[22] Industry representatives have suggested reductions in non-Annex II refunds could prompt multinational food companies to seek cheaper sources of raw materials in other countries such as Central and Eastern Europe.[23]

## United States

There has been a gradual *reduction in DPSP expenditures* over a period of years. The main reason is a growing desire by the government to reduce agricultural support expenditures in the context of reducing the Federal budget deficit. In this climate, farm programme expenditures have also come under more critical public scrutiny. Expenditures for the DPSP have fallen considerably as a share of total agricultural program expenditures. Since 1988, the purchase prices for supported dairy products have been declining in real and nominal terms. The purchase price for butter has fallen the most over this period. While the nominal cheese purchase price has only declined slightly, in real terms it has decreased steadily since 1988. In fact, since mid-1988, the wholesale cheese price has been above the purchase price for cheese. Thus, for all practical purposes, the cheese market is no longer being supported. While the same is not yet true for butter, the purchase price for butter is getting close to world market levels (US$0.65 per pound). Hence, based on these trends in purchase prices, the DPSP is *de facto* going through a gradual deregulation. This process began in 1988 when the US government began to implement decreases in the support price based on expected purchases of dairy products for the forthcoming year. Continued deregulation of the DPSP is likely since the US dairy economy will face increasing external competition in the future and because of continuing pressures to reduce government spending.

The Kaiser study considered the market-wide impacts of gradually deregulating the DPSP over the 1980-90 period. This was a period of heavy dependence on the DPSP and, therefore, the results of this study are likely to have overstated the impacts of gradual deregulation compared with the situation today. Under the gradual deregulation scenario, the purchase price for dairy products was decreased by 10 per cent per year from 1980-90. The results of this scenario followed the same pattern as immediate elimination of the DPSP, but the magnitude of change was not as large. Gradual deregulation over this period resulted in a decline in the farm milk price of 18.7 per cent, compared to a decline of 23.5 per cent under immediate elimination of the DPSP. The average loss in producer surplus under gradual deregulation over this period was 20 per cent compared with 25 per cent in the case of immediate deregulation.

In terms of wholesale prices, Kaiser found that gradual deregulation would result in a fluid price decrease of 14.7 per cent, a decrease in the frozen product prices by 8.6 per cent, a decrease in the cheese price by 5.6 per cent, and a decrease in the butter price by 39.4 per cent. Net government costs, under gradual deregulation, fell by 71 per cent, on average over the period. Gradual deregulation could also increase price instability, primarily at the farm and wholesale-processing levels. However, both farmers and processors could use the newly created (as of June 15, 1993) cheese and non-fat dry milk futures market to manage this price risk. Similar to grain farmers and processors, dairy producers and processors can use the cheese and/or non-fat dry milk futures market to hedge and/or forward contract their products.

The largest structural change on the demand side of the dairy industry is the movement away from high-fat dairy products towards *lower-fat products.* This is true with fluid milk, where consumption of low-fat and skim milk is now higher than consumption of whole milk. It is also true with manufactured products, evidenced by such recent trends as increased consumption in no-fat and low fat products, (*e.g.* cheese, sour cream, yoghurt, frozen products, and cottage cheese). This trend towards lower fat dairy products has implications for both the DPSP and milk marketing orders.

In terms of the *DPSP,* this trend has caused the government to buy more fat and less low- or non-fat products over the past several years. Industry leaders correctly point out that the United States does not have a milk-surplus problem, but rather a fat surplus problem. In response to this, the government has made substantial reductions in the purchase price for butter. At the same time, the government made an equivalent increase in the price of non-fat dry milk so that there were no adverse impacts on the price of farm milk. Since 1990, the purchase price for butter has fallen from US$1.11 per pound to US$0.65, while the purchase price for non-fat dry milk has risen from US$0.79 per pound to US$1.034. Further adjustments will likely be made in the future in response to consumer trends away from fat as long as the "tilt" of products that the CCC purchases is towards more butter relative to non fat dry milk.

*Milk marketing orders* have traditionally used fat-based pricing for raw milk with no premiums paid to farmers based on other nutritional components of milk such as protein. Fat-based pricing directly contradicts what is going on in the market place with consumers. Consequently, it is counter-productive to send farmers price signals which reward them for producing fat, while not giving them any incentives to produce other nutrients that consumers really want. Recently, some milk orders have adopted multiple component pricing plans, which pay farmers on the basis of fat and non-fat components in milk. Within five years, virtually all milk marketing orders will likely have some type of multiple component price plan in effect. If the trend away from high-fat dairy products continues, milk marketing orders will need to further adjust their pricing mechanisms to provide stronger economic incentives for farmers to produce protein and other non-fat components of milk, and stronger disincentives for fat.

As discussed in Section III, there are regional differences regarding the *modification of milk marketing orders.* Reform of milk marketing orders may be one of the key items to be debated in the dairy portion of the 1995 Farm Bill. The focus of the debate is over the regional level of Class I (fluid) prices, which basically increase with distance from the historical milk surplus area of the country (Upper Midwest). However, there are other areas of the United States that produce more milk than is consumed by the population. Consequently, some feel that the current spatial Class I price structure is not fair.

A recent study by Schiek looked at the impact of several modifications in milk marketing orders with respect to spatial Class I prices on the dairy industry, including: 1) multiple base points, 2) return to 1985 Class I price differentials, 3) and a uniform Class I price differential of US$1.80 in all regions.[24] The study suggested that none of the three options would have significant ramifications for the US dairy industry. For example, the largest impact of any policy option on any variable is the multiple base point policy's impact on producer revenue, which declines by 3.4 per cent nationally. The magnitude of impacts of all three policy scenarios tends to be about 1 per cent nationally. Regionally, producers in the North Central region of the US would be least affected under all three of the policy options, while producers in the Southeast, South Central, and Northeast are the worse off. But the magnitude of these effects are typically under 5 per cent for most regions.

The complete *elimination of milk marketing orders* has also been examined and would likely lower farm milk prices, lower wholesale and retail fluid milk prices, raise wholesale and retail manufactured milk prices, increase milk production in more efficient regions (*e.g.* West Coast and Upper Midwest), and decrease milk production in high cost areas (*e.g.* Southeast and South Central). One widely debated question regarding the complete deregulation of milk marketing orders would be the impact on market stability and monopsony power by milk processors . It was of course these concerns that, in part, led to the creation of milk marketing orders. However, conditions have changed since the early 1900s. Farms are fewer and larger, fluid markets are much larger geographically, technology can move milk across the United States, and dairy co-operatives have greater market power. These factors suggest that the market power between farmers (or co-operatives) and proprietary milk processors is much more balanced than previously. Consequently, the elimination of milk marketing orders may not open the industry to abuse of market position. On the other hand, fluid and manufactured product processors are also substantially larger and the downstream market is more highly concentrated than it was in the past. It would, therefore, be important for competition authorities to monitor dairy markets closely in order to ensure competition if the marketing orders were to be eliminated.

The United States Department of Agriculture has submitted its recommendations for policy reform which include changes to the dairy marketing programmes "to make the programme more market-oriented, protect producers financially while imposing no new burdens on consumers and taxpayers, increase (regional and international) competition, honour international trade agreements and provide environmental incentives".[25]

While noting that the cost of the dairy price support programme had fallen rapidly over the last decade, the Administration indicated the increased use of Bovine Somatotropin (BST) and import access under the Uruguay Round Agreement, coupled with no flexibility to adjust the support price downward, could cause dairy price support programme outlays and government dairy stocks to increase over the next several years.

The Administration reviewed the current price support and Federal milk marketing order programmes and offered the following examples of reform that could address these issues and respect the general objectives outlined above:

- "Change the price support programme to avoid any prospect for accumulation of Government dairy stocks. For example, in exchange for reducing dairy marketing assessments, the milk price support level could be phased down.
- Revise marketing order authorities to reduce incentives for excessive milk production and to encourage regional competition. This could entail broader scope or flexibility in marketing order authorities to make industry-consensus changes through administrative procedures. Some examples include phasing down the minimum differential for milk used as fluid or revising statutory authority to permit adoption of an alternative order structure, such as multiple basing points.
- Encourage environmentally beneficial practices by dairy farmers. A broader set of dairy farmers in threatened and impaired watersheds could be required to adopt measures that advance desirable environmental objectives, such as confined animal waste handling procedures. These new compliance costs could be partially offset through mechanisms such as grants to small farmers and low interest loans."

The Federal Agricultural Improvement and Reform (FAIR) Act would eliminate the current levy on dairy producers in 1996 and phase down support price for butter, milk powder and cheese from 1996 to 1999, to be replaced, at the end of 1999, by a recourse loan programme set at US$218 per tonne of milk equivalent. The dairy Export Incentive Program would remain with the maximum volume and funding levels permitted under GATT. The number of milk marketing orders should be reduced from 33 to no more than 14 and no less than 10 in 3 years.

## Canada

A number of policy reforms have been introduced in Canada over the last several years aimed at moving towards a more integrated and market responsive dairy industry. One such change has been a **reduction in the direct subsidy** paid from a total of approximately C$ 270 million (pre-1988) to C$ 225 million in 1994. The federal government pays dairy farmers a direct subsidy for industrial milk produced within domestic requirements. A reduced rate of direct subsidy to dairy farmers has been applied so that no impact results on total returns received by farmers. Thus, processors have to pay more for milk. This has resulted in higher prices for cheese and other processed dairy products.

It has been estimated that, as a result of this reduction as implemented by the Canadian Dairy Commission, there is no great effect on production or consumption, the skim milk powder support price increases, the butter support price remains constant, and cheese and other dairy product prices rise slightly due to the increase in industrial milk price to processors. There is a slight reduction in consumption of skim milk powder, cheese and other dairy products due to these higher product prices and there has been a small net reduction in domestic requirement for industrial milk leading to a small decrease in market share quota (MSQ).

The 1995 federal budget included a further 30 per cent reduction in the direct subsidy over two years (*i.e.* to C$ 4.62/hl in 1995/96 and to C$ 3.80/hl in 1996/97). As a result, the value of the subsidy will fall to C$ 160 million by 1997/98. The 1996 federal budget included a five-year phase out of the subsidy, commencing on 1 August 1997. The Government has launched consultations with the dairy industry on how best to use the subsidies previously paid to producers to support the long-term growth of the sector in the new trading environment.

Another policy change has been applying any support price increase to *skim milk powder prices.* Historically, target price increases were shared evenly by butter and skim milk powder support prices. Since 1990, only skim milk powder support prices have been increased. The effect of this change was an increase in the demand for butter and a reduction in demand for skim milk powder. In addition, two rebate programmes (funded by producer levies) were introduced aimed at stimulating butterfat demand by processors. These rebate programs have lowered the cost of processed dairy products inputs (*e.g.* butter and cheese) to further processors, thereby stimulating consumption of these inputs by the further processing sector. Overall, MSQ (in butterfat equivalents) dropped from 1990 to 1993 with declining domestic demand but has recently stabilised.

Similarly, *multiple component pricing* (MCP) was introduced to permit all components of milk to be measured and valued to reflect market demands. Since 1992, four provinces have introduced multiple component pricing for industrial milk (Ontario, Quebec, Manitoba and New Brunswick). Initial component prices for butterfat, protein and other solids were selected such that overall returns for milk of average composition was unchanged. Multiple component pricing is not expected to have a large immediate impact on returns or milk supplies. Depending on the relative prices set, MCP could have a long-run impact on the composition of milk produced in Canada. If component prices are set with market demands in mind then pricing and resulting milk allocation and processed product mix will move closer to market trends. If component prices are set to maintain producer revenues then such allocative improvements may not be achieved.

Provincial restrictions on quota holdings by individual producers and federal upper limits on subsidy eligibility are being gradually reduced. Past limits on the amount of quota held by any one producer have either been removed or raised to levels well above current farm size. Most within-province restrictions of quota movements, originally imposed to protect dairy production in higher cost regions of a province have been removed although, in some provinces, regulations require that quota be purchased with the farm and that the farm must be operated by the new owner-operator for a period of at least one year. The greatest constraint to dairy farm size expansion, however, remains the lack of availability of quota.

A number of provinces (Manitoba, Saskatchewan, New Brunswick, Ontario) have now adopted a *single quota for fluid and industrial milk.* Many other provinces are considering changing to a single quota system. In addition to reduced administration costs, a single quota implies that all producers receive the same price for their in quota milk (essentially a means of sharing access to all market uses equally among all producers). The single quota system has no major effects on aggregate quantities and prices but there could be significant individual impacts on producers whose relative holdings of fluid and industrial milk quotas vary from the provincial average. The impact could be positive or negative depending on whether an individual's industrial quota percentage was above or below the provincial average. How the change is implemented/compensated for in each province will affect the magnitude of these impacts.

The administrative adjustments undertaken in moving to a single, within province quota differ by province but in all cases an "income-neutral" approach was used to compensate individual dairy producers. The system adopted in the province of Ontario provides a typical example. As in all provinces, the former Ontario system had two types of quota, one for fluid milk and one for industrial milk, with fluid milk prices above those for milk used in processing. Individual producers generally held both types of quota although the proportions would vary and revenue on a per unit basis would be higher for deliveries of fluid milk. The new system was designed to place all producers on an equal footing while increasing industry market responsiveness and reducing administrative complexities. Fluid and industrial quotas were replaced by a single quota issued in kilograms of butter fat. The conversion process involved adjustments at the individual producer level so that producers with a high proportion of fluid milk quota would receive additional "pooled" quota to compensate for the lower average price while producers with a greater proportion of industrial quota would have their quota reduced. Over 86 per cent of producers had a quota adjustment of less than 2 per cent.[26]

The movement to a single quota for fluid and industrial milk was, in part, aimed at reducing the pressures of MSQ cuts on quota prices. In response to declining domestic demand and growing surpluses of butter (which was being exported with subsidies financed through producer levies), it had been necessary to occasionally reduce the industrial milk MSQ. As farmers MSQ declined, demand for industrial and fluid milk quota coming onto the market increased, causing quota prices to rise. Many farmers found themselves in effect "repurchasing" quota several times as they bought additional quota from retiring farmers to replace that eroded by successive quota reductions simply to maintain the same level of production.

A next logical stage in the reform process would be a single national market for quota. The single quota system at the provincial level is seen as a step towards a national system of supply control in Canada. A recent study by the Ministry of Agriculture concluded that unification of the Canadian market under one system would allow improved economic efficiency as a result of increased interprovincial competition and free movement of quota across Canada.[27] Production and processing could be expected to relocate to the areas of greatest comparative advantage. Such a change would also provide an opportunity to review a number of existing provincial policies including, controls on wholesale and retail prices of fluid milk, plant supply quotas and end-use pricing.

In late 1994, a dairy industry Task Force representing all levels of the food chain made a number of recommendations to increase industry market responsiveness and competitiveness including the pooling of market returns from all milk classes. To date, six provinces (Prince Edward Island, New Brunswick, Nova Scotia, Quebec, Ontario and Manitoba) have agreed to *pool revenues* from all milk (fluid and industrial). A similar arrangement between the provinces of British Columbia, Alberta and Saskatchewan is under discussion. Since the price paid to producers for fluid milk is considerably higher than that for industrial milk, those provinces with a high proportion of fluid milk (*e.g.* 40 per cent in Ontario) will experience a decline in the average pooled price whereas provinces with a low proportion of fluid milk (*e.g.* 20 per cent in Quebec) will experience an increase. Arrangements have been worked out between provinces for a one-time compensatory payment to address the loses (*e.g.* Quebec will pay C\$ 14 million into the pooled fund).

Policy reforms under discussion include more **market-oriented pricing** for food ingredients. Alternatives to the current cost of production pricing schemes appear necessary. In fact, the Canadian Dairy Commission has moved in this direction. Responding to the decline in butter demand and the high cost of exporting butter surpluses, the Canadian Dairy Commission reduced prices for surplus butter if used in the domestic baking industry. Other price rebates on milk and particular end uses have been given to processors. These rebates, in turn, reduce the net prices paid to farmers. Also, while there is little expectation of significant trade pressures arising from the current UR Agreement, it is recognised that some movement towards greater trade liberalisation is likely and there is concern that high cost producers would not be able to compete. Gradual adjustments now, before border protection is reduced/eliminated, are seen as an alternative to rapid price declines in the future.

As of August 1, 1995, the dairy producer levy system was modified. The producer levy system, which was used to finance exports, was replaced by a system of special milk classes, the revenues from which will be pooled among all Canadian dairy farmers. Nine provinces (Newfoundland is not part of the national marketing plan) agreed to replace the Dairy Export Assistance Programme, Further Processors Rebate Programme and the Butterfat Utilisation Programme with a special *low-priced milk class* (the Basic Formula Price, BFP will be used as the reference price for Canadian producers) which should allow processors and exporters to improve their competitiveness in international and domestic high value-added markets.

The policy reforms undertaken in Canada to date have been largely aimed at a reinstumentation of the current supply management system. However, the need for/ benefits of more fundamental reforms are beginning to receive greater attention. Continued government support of the sector is coming under increasing pressure because of the relative importance of the sector to the general economy, concerns about the lack of international competitiveness of the sector and resource pressures caused by governments' deficits and debt.

As access to Canadian dairy markets increases, and tariff levels decrease, the scope of domestic supply controls will diminish. Movement towards a more liberal regime will bring about gradual reductions in the value of quotas. While faster and more substantial reform initiatives could have a more significant impact on farm asset levels, particularly the market value of production quota, the foregoing discussion of policy impacts suggests significant benefits could be achieved from adjustments over a shorter period. However, a more rapid reform process may increase the need for complementary adjustment programmes to help offset the costs of reform along the lines of those provided in the context of the recent removal of the grain transportation subsidy.

*New Zealand*

The New Zealand dairy industry has a very low level of government intervention and it has continued to grow despite a high level of price variability and total exposure to world markets. The domestic market for dairy products is now deregulated and there are no import barriers. The one significant area of government involvement in the industry is the legislation which allows the New Zealand Dairy Board to be the sole exporter of dairy products. The Board is not supported by any government funding and all financial responsibility is vested in the dairy producers, but they do have some reporting requirements to the government. The discussion below describes some of the alternative approaches which could be used to remove the remaining intervention which exist in the New Zealand dairy industry.

The government could move towards *liberalising entitlement to export* by allowing processing companies greater access to international markets. The NZDB already allows direct exports of approved dairy products. These are largely specialised products destined for consumer markets and require the approval of marketing plans by the board. Measures of this activity are not widely available but the board is now required to report on such approvals to the government.

Liberalising exports could allow such activity without approval by the Board and there might be some attempt to define the type of products which might be exported by the Board or the companies. The attraction of such a proposal would be that the individual processing companies could focus on specialised products which are highly differentiated, and the Board could market less differentiated bulk products where there is more likely to be gains from price discrimination in world markets. The difficulties in this proposal would come from such issues as defining the range of products and determining whether the Board would be required to market all of the product supplied.

It is most likely that the current process of gradual liberalisation will be continued under the control of the Board but large scale activity of this type could also produce conflict with the increasing level of consumer marketing by the Board. Although international firms are currently able to make direct investments in processing milk if they wish to, and there is no obstacle for dairy farmers to supply them, it is difficult to know to which extent they will use the opportunities.

One proposal which has been widely discussed is to *privatise the NZDB* by removing its statutory powers and allocating shares in the organisation to the existing producers. The current legislation clarifies that the Board is owned by the dairy farmers through their ownership of the processing co-operatives. This would make it a relatively simple process to allocate shares which could be traded either amongst farmers or to other investors. The advantage of this process is that the Board and its marketing expertise remain intact in the short term, and the co-operatives have the choice of continuing to export through the board. Alternatively, they could choose to export as individual firms or enter into marketing arrangements with other firms. An amendment to the Dairy Board's empowering legislation is currently before Parliament. The amendment will restructure the New Zealand Dairy Board into a co-operative marketing company owned by New Zealand's dairy processing co-operatives in proportion to the product they supply to it. In addition, it will change the dissolution provisions to ensure that the New Zealand Dairy Board is a going concern in the event of a removal of its statutory powers. The amendment does not propose to change the New Zealand Dairy Board's statutory powers.

To the extent that the NZDB could effectively market the dairy products and retain the confidence of all of the individual firms, the Board could continue to operate as at present with the same economic benefits. This action would have the effect of placing the processing companies in the position of the monitors of the efficiency of the Board. The size and marketing expertise of some firms such as NZ Dairy Group (45 per cent of production) would suggest that they would be the most likely to become independent of the Board, but other firms that have established markets for specialised products might also benefit from independent exporting or developing marketing arrangements with international firms.

An alternative scenario is that the Board itself could become more selective in the purchasing of milk products. Without the requirement to purchase all of the export milk products, there would be potential for the new organisation to increase the level of international products purchased and to move into a wider range of food products. This creates the possibility of forming a multinational food processing firm which is at least initially owned by New Zealand producers.

One concern which has been raised is the ownership of the rents from any voluntary quotas that are currently controlled by the Board. In principle these could be retained by the new organisation and transferred to the shareholders or suppliers, but there would be a case for ensuring that they are shared by other exporters. This could be done in a manner that is common in other exporting industries where quota rights are allocated on the basis of the share of New Zealand production.

Another possible complication is the current allocation of ownership through the co-operative firms. This could limit the individual producers control over the total assets and would mean that they are dependent on the policies of their individual co-operative. However, it might also create more stability for the restructured organisation and the processing companies could own shares without trading with the organisation.

It should be noted that in April 1995 the Board moved to establish a financial structure that allocates shares to the co-operatives in an attempt to consolidate the ownership structure and to allow dividends to be paid. This does not change fundamentally the export control arrangements but should allow a clarification of the returns from different sources. It is too early to be clear about the long run impacts but the change should meet some concerns in this area.

A further alternative is for the government to require the *dissolution of the NZDB*. This is probably unlikely and unnecessary if the objective of the deregulation would be to remove the statutory control over exports and not to completely remove the co-operative marketing organisation. A major complication in such a strategy would be the disposal of the assets of the existing Board. It would be easier to sell these assets to be sold if the existing ownership were vested in the government, but this would require a change in the recent amendments to the Acts.

In any of the cases where the board does not remain fully representative of the industry it would be likely that a new producer controlled organisation would remain in place to represent the interests of producers. Such an organisation would be equivalent to those existing in other industries, and would probably have responsibility for activities such as generic promotion and research.

## EU Dairy Regime under the CAP

The EU Agriculture Commissioner has recently outlined some of the pressures for reform facing the CAP, stressing the need to continue along the road of reduced government support initiated with the 1992 CAP reforms.[28] Given the *Uruguay Round commitments,* there is a need to move towards exporting without subsidies in order to participate in the growth of world markets. New GATT/WTO negotiations to begin in 2000 are likely to further liberalise trade, requiring even more adjustments in EU agriculture in response to increasing international competition in foreign and domestic markets. Continued market price support could be expected to result in additional supply controls which would be difficult to achieve with international commitments to greater market access, suggesting that a separation of market policies and income support would be more sustainable in the long-run. In an earlier speech to the International Dairy Federation, the Commissioner recognised the pressures to rebalance demand and supply in the dairy sector, suggesting that the EU needs to adjust its dairy policy to cater to the new world trade agreement and to allow east European dairy industries to be integrated into the EU dairy market.

In fact, the 1992 CAP reform has not had a significant impact on the dairy regime. The Commission originally proposed a 15 per cent cut in butter prices and 5 per cent cut in SMP support prices over three years with direct compensation payments to dairy producers. The intervention price for butter has been reduced by 6 per cent (7.3 per cent taking into account the agrimonetary adjustment) but there have been no cuts in the intervention price for SMP since 1993. The Commission proposed to cut quotas by two per cent in both 1993/94 and 1994/95 but, on the basis of reports on market situation indicating that the European Union can fulfil its Uruguay Round commitments without reducing the quota, the Council decided to reject these cuts. Moreover, there was a commitment in the 1994 CAP price fixing that there would be no quota cuts in 1995/96.[29]

While the EU dairy regime is still based on the traditional CAP mechanisms of market intervention and subsidised exports with the addition in 1984 of *production controls,* programmes for most other major commodities have been modified to incorporate direct subsidisation of producers combined with declining market support. The imposition of quotas in 1984 stabilised dairy production at levels 13-15 per cent over domestic requirements while price levels have been maintained well above world prices. The dairy regime continues to be a large budgetary burden. Total expenditure on the EU dairy regime was 4.2 billion ECU in 1994 and 4.0 billion ECU in 1995, down from the 6.0 billion ECU levels of 1985 and 1988 as expenditures on export subsidies and subsidised disposal schemes fall. This makes it the third most expensive support regime after arable crops (14.6 billion ECU) and beef (4.9 billion ECU).[30]

The underlying problem is that the EU dairy industry produces more milk than can be sold either domestically or on the international market without subsidies, although quotas have generally stabilised the level of production and intervention stocks of butter and SMP have come down significantly. For the EU-15, dairy production remains 14-15 million tonnes more than the domestic market can absorb and the excess is *exported with subsidies* which represent about 50 per cent of the total dairy sector budget. Domestic consumption is also sustained through further internal subsidies (*e.g.* the SMP feed incorporation scheme, diversion of butter to food manufacturers). which largely contribute to supporting domestic market prices

These subsidies create distortions in the processing sector as dairies have been prepared to pay high prices for milk in order to secure supplies to produce dairy products which are often surplus to domestic demand. Under current strong market conditions, EU countries are exporting more dairy products now than in 1983 (the new Member states at the time, Spain and Portugal, were dairy deficit countries) but world markets are highly volatile. The Commission warned of this market instability in its 1994 report on the state of the dairy market, stressing the unfavourable situation in Eastern Europe and the Middle East, rising production and subsidised exports from the US and increased production in Oceania.[31]

Growing concerns over the impact of dairy policy on the processing sector have been expressed by a number of key dairy industry representatives, in particular with regard to future *export refunds*.[32] Nevertheless, the share of EU dairy exports without refunds might continue to increase especially for cheese. Moreover, to develop new markets, the EU processing industry would shift to contracts with suppliers outside of the Union (with access to cheaper raw materials) to produce their branded products. Besides, quota restrictions are seen as restraints on downstream investment as it is difficult for processors to justify major new investment when there is little prospect of increasing output. Although the EU dairy industry has often been in the forefront for developing new markets, it has been argued that without dairy policy reform the EU may forfeit valuable markets; foregoing the opportunity of exploiting new markets in developing countries and missing out on product and market development opportunities which new foreign consumers are expected to stimulate.

An assessment of the prospects of the EU dairy industry in the view of one investment analyst was not optimistic, concluding that the EU "produces too much raw milk at too high a price to sustain a strong dairy industry".[33] According to this assessment, potential investors would be concerned that short-term favourable market conditions for longer life dairy products outside the EU were distracting the industry from necessary restructuring and that the industry would have difficulty attracting investors until medium-term prospects improved which, it was suggested, would require lower real input costs, higher gross margins and more leverage of processors over channels of distribution. More competitive trading conditions were seen as a potential catalyst for this type of structural adjustment.

A number of policy reforms to address the pressures discussed above have been advanced for discussion. The most common options include *reductions in support price levels, reductions in quotas and a two-tier quota system.* Price cuts would be the most attractive option for the processing industry but would have to be substantial to reduce output or to enhance the ability to export without subsidies (a figure close to the 30 per cent cut imposed in the cereal sector in the 1993-96 period has been suggested) and the potential cost of compensation in the form of direct income support would be very high if full compensation for price cuts were considered.[34] Quota reductions would have a more direct impact on levels of production (and budgetary expenditure) but could raise the prices of dairy products and dairy quotas while further restricting development of the processing sector, possibly leading to loss of markets and some relocation of processing.

A number of variations of a double price system (similar to the EU sugar regime) with ''B'' quota for milk used for processing into products for export without subsidy have been proposed. This approach is seen by some as a means of maintaining support levels for producers while allowing the industry to remain competitive on world markets. The main concerns about the double price system is that non-subsidised exports of ''B'' dairy products would compete with subsidised exports of ''A'' dairy products, that the system should be made compatible with GATT and that, because of the large number of dairies and wide range of products, it would be relatively complex to manage.

## United Kingdom

The main UK policy instrument examined in this section is the **milk marketing system.** This is because of its significant impact on downstream industries and because the system has recently been changed. However, the pressures for reform of the EU Common Agricultural Policy (CAP), described above, will have a major impact on the UK dairy sector. As discussed in Annex 1, agricultural support in the EU has been based primarily on market price support provided through institutional prices, variable import levies and export subsidies. For dairy products, these policies have been operated since 1984 in conjunction with quotas that limit the volume of production on which support applies, with heavy penalties for milk in excess of quota.

At present, the UK dairy industry is going through a period of adjustment to the new marketing arrangements following the abolition of the Milk Marketing Boards. Although Milk Marque has acquired some 50 per cent of milk sales in the United Kingdom, it will be subject to competition legislation and the threat of action by the Monopolies and Mergers Commission if it abuses its market power. Furthermore, the changes have brought to an end a pricing system which protected inefficient processors, restricted innovation and hindered the development of value-added processing (the UK has been exporting low value-added products such as skimmed milk powder and importing high value fresh milk products such as yoghurts).

It is too early to assess the effects of the new marketing system, which is in its first years of operation. However, the government made it clear that it will monitor the situation to ensure that there is no abuse of **market power.** Certainly, producer prices have increased significantly under the new arrangements, reflecting a number of factors. The old system prevented the allocation of milk to its most profitable use and, inevitably, some processors were prepared to outbid their competitors to claim a larger share of the domestic milk supply which is limited by quota. Also many milk processing companies, certainly the larger ones, wanted to source milk direct from farmers to ensure security, continuity and quality. To achieve this, premiums, up to 24 pence per litre (*i.e.* 10 per cent higher than previous prices) were being offered as well as other bonus incentives.

The auction system, by which Milk Marque sells milk, has been subject to some criticism because it has forced companies to bid high prices to ensure continuity of supply. Recently Milk Marque has modified this system, added to which, the proportion of "non-guaranteed" supplies can be obtained much more cheaply. Ultimately, the milk price is constrained by the ability of companies to source from abroad or locate in other member states. It would not be in the interests of Milk Marque to encourage such a reaction or to provoke intervention by the UK or EU competition authorities.

The initial effect on farmers of the reforms will be their effect on *average milk prices.* However, there could be longer term implications for pricing and production patterns. Already, there is increasing interest in price differentials to reflect quality, composition and volume but it remains the case that prices do not fully reflect location. In this more competitive market, it is possible that buyers will seek out those producers situated near to processing and manufacturing plants where transport costs would be lower. This will encourage a more spatially efficient distribution of dairy farming.

It is likely that there will be some *consolidation of manufacturing* in response to several factors: the abolition of formula pricing and the protection it provided; competition from an increasingly European dairy sector which views the market as European or even global, rather than national or local; and competition from retailers in own-label supplies, but most importantly in the lucrative liquid milk market. Already this year, Northern Foods, the largest door-step delivery company, has announced plans for about 1 000 redundancies in its milk bottling and distribution operations. It is also calling for the regional division of the door-step delivery market (*i.e.* the creation of regional monopolies). Although the reason put forward is one of increased efficiency, it reflects to a large extent the growing sales of fresh milk through supermarkets and the steady decline in doorstep delivery.

Deregulation has meant an end to market distortions created by the system of end-use pricing and has already lead to a general upward movement in producer prices as processors have competed for the UK's limited milk supply. However, there is little evidence that these prices are out of line with prices in other parts of the Community. The competitive behaviour of Milk Marque will be closely monitored even though its share of the domestic market is not out of line with that of producer co-operatives in some other member states. Efficient spatial allocation implies hardship for some, possibly demanding support on regional development or social grounds. Likewise, consolidation of processing could create difficulties for small firms, an area of industrial policy in which the EU has been paying particular attention.

### The Netherlands

The EU dairy policy under the CAP is also the major policy regime impacting on the dairy sector in the Netherlands. Thus, the pressures for *reform of the CAP* dairy regime (as discussed above) will in turn influence pressures for structural adjustment in the

Netherlands. Along with the UK, France and Germany, the Netherlands is one of the major dairy producing (and exporting) countries of the Union such that changes to the nature and/or level of support to the dairy sector would have a significant impact on the agricultural economy.

Cheese exports are of particular importance to the Netherland's dairy sector, accounting for about 22 per cent of total EU cheese exports marketed in 130 countries. The Dutch industry sees it as desirable to maintain its current world market position, and because of **GATT restraints** on subsidised exports, this implies growing pressures to become less reliant on exporting with subsidies. At present, the EU exports about 50 000 tonnes of non-subsidised cheese. Processors are likely to respond by focusing more on evolving products with the greatest value-added. Some industry experts have suggested the total volume of exports could be maintained and possibly enlarged by eliminating the refunds on exports to "wealthy" countries, while continuing subsidised exports to more price-sensitive markets.

Quota purchase and lease prices for milk in the Netherlands are the highest in the EU (Table 7). Originally the producers were strongly opposed to the quota system. However, the relatively free **transfer of quota** and the high demand for production rights has resulted in substantial investments by the larger expanding farms in additional quota and windfall gains for all dairy farms through the capitalisation of production rents. For 1993/94, the number of transactions was estimated at 1 000 for the quota transfers of a whole farm, 6 000 for partial quota sales and 12 000 for quota leases. As a result, considerable resistance among Dutch dairy producers to any policy reform that reduced the value of quota would be likely and, in such an event, demands for compensation would be extremely high.

**Budgetary pressures** have also increased the public debate on policy reform. In 1994 the Dutch turned from a position of being a net recipient from FEOGA (CAP funding) to one of being a net contributor. In 1995 the Netherlands' net contribution was

Table 7.   **Purchase and lease prices paid for quota, 1994/95**[1]

|  | Quota Purchase Price (Gld per kg) | Quota Lease Price (Gld per kg) |
| --- | --- | --- |
| United Kingdom | 1.62 | 0.38 |
| France [2] | 0.40 | n.a. |
| Denmark | 0.56 | 0.11 |
| Germany | 0.94 | 0.05 |
| Netherlands | 4.00 | 0.36 |
| Belgium | 2.06 | 0.16 |

n.a.:  not available.
1.   Due to low milk production in some countries (Belgium, Germany) in 1994/95, farmers anticipated an equalisation payment at year end which reduced interest in leasing quota.
2.   Purchase price for France based on price paid in last cessation scheme.
*Source:*   J. B van Dijk (1995), *Milk Quota Transfers in Six EU Member States*, unpublished mimeograph, Wageningen Agricultural University, the Netherlands, February.

0.4 billion ECU and is expected to increase further. Figures for the total FEOGA budget are shown in Table 8. The Ministry of Finance expects that in 1995, with 0.7 per cent of its GDP, the Netherlands will become the largest contributor in terms of GDP share to the EU budget as a whole, including structural funds. This has created additional fiscal pressures in the Netherlands and the Government has responded by advocating a more market-oriented approach to agriculture and reduced government intervention. The dairy sector is by far the greatest beneficiary of the share of total receipts under FEOGA attributed to the Netherlands, accounting for 48.2 per cent of agricultural receipts in 1992, 54.3 per cent in 1993 and 59.6 per cent in 1995. Government forecasts up to the year 1999 suggest a continuation of the trend towards increased payments, adding further pressure for policy reform.

*Environmental pressures* in the Netherlands have led to restrictions on intensive agriculture in the form of the maximum use of minerals per hectare. Farmers have initiated environmental co-operatives and collective approaches to manure processing to address the problems on a regional basis but these efforts have been only moderately successful. Most farmers are attempting to deal with the government restrictions on an individual basis. This generally involves acquiring more land, feeding more roughage or by making contracts with crop farmers for disposal of manure or slurry. One consequence is that more land input is required to produce the product. This approach has led to pressures on the land market, generating higher farm land prices.

By the year 2010 all mineral and ammonia surpluses will have to be brought down to acceptable levels. To keep the socio-economic consequences for farmers within limits, environmental standards for agriculture will be tightened gradually. A number of proposals are currently being debated regarding the emission of nitrates and phosphates. As farmers see the different measures as being very expensive, environmental groups have argued that there is simply too many cattle in the Netherlands. They state that the environmental pressure from agriculture can not be brought back to reasonable levels without decreasing total livestock production.

Table 8.  **Total FEOGA payments and receipts in the Netherlands**

ECU billions

|  | Net position | Total payments | Total receipts |
|---|---|---|---|
| 1980 | +0.6 | 0.9 | 1.5 |
| 1985 | +0.5 | 1.5 | 2.0 |
| 1990 | +1.2 | 1.7 | 2.9 |
| 1993 | +0.1 | 2.2 | 2.3 |
| 1994 | −0.2 | 2.1 | 1.9 |
| 1995 | −0.4 | 2.3 | 1.9 |
| 1999 (forecast) | −0.9 | 2.7 | 1.8 |

*Source:*   For years 1980-1993, *Annual Report of the European Accounting Office*; for years 1994,1995 and 1999 forecast, reports of Dutch Ministry of Finance and Ministry of Agriculture, Nature Management and Fisheries.

As agri-environmental policies become more stringent, environmental rather than market restrictions could increasingly determine production capacity and the costs associated with their implementation are likely to rise with implications for the competitiveness and growth of the Netherlands dairy industry. The distribution of environmental costs along the food chain will likely emerge as an issue. Recently, for example, German milk producers and processors complained that the costs of the environmental "green dot" scheme were one-sided at the expense of the dairy industry; that some of the cost had not been shifted to the retail trade and consumers as originally intended.[35]

Finally, there is considerable debate in the Netherlands over the future role of *public institutions* in the areas of agricultural research, education and extension. Extension and most applied lines of research have already been privatised. Research on new product and market development, which was carried out using collective funds by the Netherlands Institute of Dairy Research, is increasingly being privatised. With a much more concentrated structure and a shift from institutional to consumer markets, the large Dutch dairy co-operatives, private firms and limited companies are now less supportive of government-directed generic production and market research, preferring internal funding of more market-oriented research and development.

## V.  Summary and conclusions

This paper attempts to examine the impacts of dairy policy on the structure and performance of the dairy industry as a whole. The impetus for this broader agro-food approach comes from the recognition that intra-industry linkages within the food chain can affect the outcomes of agricultural policies and that these policies, generally directed at the farm level, can also influence the structure and performance of upstream and downstream industries. The objective of the paper is not to provide a comprehensive assessment of dairy policy for individual countries but rather to provide an overview of the kinds of impacts that have been observed across a range of policy approaches and institutional arrangements, with particular reference to downstream processing. Some of the policy reforms underway or under consideration are also reviewed.

Dairy policy in five countries are examined, including the *United States, Canada, New Zealand,* the *United Kingdom* and the *Netherlands.* With the exception of New Zealand, the level of government intervention in the dairy industry remains significant. The major instruments of *US* dairy policy are dairy price supports and milk marketing orders, which set regional prices and influence milk moving into various marketing channels. *Canada* provides support through a comprehensive supply management system, using production controls and price supports. In the *United Kingdom* and the *Netherlands*, dairy producers are covered under the EU Common Agricultural Policy (CAP) which uses administered pricing and intervention buying as a means of price support, with quotas introduced in 1984 to restrict production. Until recently, *UK* producers had to sell milk through the Milk Marketing Boards and all processors had to buy milk from the Boards. A system of production quotas and price controls had been in place for liquid milk in *New Zealand* prior to 1987.

Much of the current dairy policy has it origins in the 1930s, when milk prices were severely depressed. Policies were introduced to stabilise milk prices, raise farm incomes and provide producers with greater bargaining power against downstream processors. Over time policy objectives were modified to encompass such goals as protection of the family farm, rural employment opportunities, reasonable consumer prices and increased productivity. More recently, reduced government expenditures, improved economic efficiency and increased market orientation have been added to the list of policy goals. These multiple objectives, often poorly defined and conflicting, make the task of assessing policy effectiveness difficult.

Moreover, the structure of the industry has changed significantly in the intervening period. Some of the original justifications for dairy policy may no longer be valid. Farms are fewer and larger, milk markets are more geographically dispersed, technology can transport milk further and faster and dairy co-operatives have much more market power. Recent OECD work on farm employment and farm household incomes suggest a declining dependence on agricultural activities alone as a component of total farm household income, with a greater share of labour hours devoted to off-farm employment.[36] Another consequence of structural adjustment, as evidenced by OECD work on the transfer efficiency of agricultural policy, is that only a small share of the money resulting from price support may translate into increased farm household incomes.[37]

Available evidence suggests that dairy policy in the *United States, Canada, the United Kingdom and The Netherlands* (as could be expected in other countries where government intervention is high and based on market price support) has had a range of impacts on industry structure and performance. Dairy policies, for the most part, have been successful in maintaining farm incomes and stabilising domestic markets although less effective in achieving some of the more socially-oriented objectives such as maintaining family farms. For example, structural adjustment in the dairy industry has kept pace, and often exceeded, that of other commodity sectors, which also means that dairy farms could now be still viable with less support. Moreover, the costs to consumers and taxpayers are high and there are significant unintended impacts on downstream processing. A number of the studies cited suggest some elements of the dairy policies examined have contributed to economic efficiency losses, for example, in the allocation of resources, milk and dairy product surpluses and, in some cases, regional distortions in production and processing. In terms of policy impacts on industry performance, various studies on countries reviewed here identified a number of negative effects including higher consumer prices, constraints on productivity growth, reduced market responsiveness, focus on domestic markets, under-utilisation of plant capacity, lack of incentives for value-added innovation, and reduced international competitiveness. Nevertheless, it should be noted that, in some other countries, despite constraining dairy policies, the dairy industry was able to diversify its activities, to innovate and to adjust to markets, improving therefore its international competitiveness.

Monetary transfers to the dairy industry from taxpayers and domestic consumers as a result of dairy policies, as measured by producer subsidy equivalents (PSE) and consumer subsidy equivalents (CSE), are large. Estimates of the dairy PSE for 1994 at US$49.8 billion and the dairy CSE at US$38.0 billion for the OECD as a whole, in both cases representing about 30 per cent of total monetary transfers to agriculture. Percentage

PSEs and CSEs, which measure monetary transfers as a proportion of the value of production (or consumption), are significantly higher for dairy than for other agricultural commodities in most Member countries, with transfers exceeding 60-70 per cent of the value of production (or consumption) in many cases.

Reductions in levels of support for the dairy industry resulting from commitments under the UR Agreement will not be significant in the short-run. A comparison of the *ad valorem* equivalents (AVE) of the base tariff rates with those based on price-gap estimates for some OECD countries suggests that, in general, the base rate AVE has been set significantly above the market price support AVE. Initial tariff rates for skim milk powder and butter, for example, have been set at levels that would not appear to require significant reductions in support even after the initial phase-in period. Further, dairy products figure prominently in the producer categories subject to the minimum (15 per cent) reduction per tariff line under country UR Agreement commitments. However, these commitments will in time contribute to a lessening of production and trade distortions in dairy markets and to improvements in the allocation of resources in the dairy industry.

More immediate reform initiatives are coming from domestic pressures for change. A desire to assist the industry to adapt to changing consumer demands, such as increased demand for low-fat and new value-added products, means removing or altering policies that mask market signals. Static domestic dairy markets have the industry looking at exports as an avenue for growth but this can only occur through international competitiveness which can be hindered by policies contributing to economic inefficiency. Similarly, concerns over anticipated increases in foreign competition in domestic markets are leading policy-makers to re-evaluate the impact of policies on industry structure and performance. New technologies in production, transportation and processing are changing the structure of the industry and reducing the effectiveness of policies developed under different circumstances. Growing environmental concern and increased awareness of the linkages between agriculture and the environment have led to additional constraints on production and processing. Perhaps most importantly, budgetary pressures, common to all Member countries, are forcing governments to reassess the levels of support to the dairy industry.

For the most part, the approach to dairy policy reform has been one of reinstrumentation, a gradual adjustment for existing policies to reduce programme costs, promote economic efficiency and improve industry market orientation. Exceptionally, *New Zealand* has undergone fundamental policy reform, resulting in a dairy industry with no direct income support programmes, no market price supports and no import controls but does maintain the Dairy Board which acts as a single-seller for dairy exports. Notwithstanding the obvious benefits of substantial reform for the agro-food sector as a whole, the weak justification for much of the continuing intervention and the high cost of support, complete and sudden deregulation may be perceived to be difficult in many countries. The disruption that could result from the abolition of long standing policy regimes if production were to respond more directly to market signals and the demands for compensation by those affected may be seen as having high short-term costs. However, maintaining the existing policy environment and risking the long-run economic health of the sector is equally undesirable. In such cases, one option may be targeted adjustment measures to help offset short-term costs. Nevertheless, gradual policy reform can lead to some improvements in the form of programme cost reductions, gains in economic efficiency and greater market orientation.

# Notes and references

1. OECD/GD(94)58, "Structural Change in the Dairy Sector of OECD Countries: Recent Trends and Implications for Policies", Paris, pp. 27-28, 1994.

2. For a recent discussion of the two-way relationship between structural change in the food chain and food policy intervention see Spencer Henson, Rupert Loader and Bruce Traill (1995), "Contemporary Food Policy Issues and the Food Supply Chain", *European Review of Agricultural Economics,* Volume 22-3, pp. 271-281.

3. Four country-specific consultancies assessing the impact of government intervention on their respective dairy industries provide much of the background material for this report. The consultants included Dr. Harry Kaiser, Department of Agriculture Economics and Managerial Economics, Cornell University (United States), Dr. Anthony Zwart, Department of Economics and Marketing, Lincoln University (New Zealand), Dr. Bruce Traill, Department of Agricultural Economics and Marketing, University of Reading (United Kingdom) and Dr. Gert van Dijk, The Agricultural University , Wageningen (Netherlands). In addition, an unpublished report on Canadian dairy policy was provided by the federal ministry, Agriculture and Agri-Food Canada.

4. OECD (1994), *Dairy Sector Indicators*, Paris, p. 32.

5. Agra Europe (1995), (London), *Commission to Recommend Dairy Policy Changes,* September 15, P/1.

6. This also applies to New Zealand co-operatives.

7. Marchant, M. (1993*), Political Economic analysis of US Dairy Policies and European Community Dairy Policy Comparisons,* Garland Publishing, Inc., New York and London, p. 88.

8. OECD (1983), *Positive Adjustment Policies in the Dairy Sector,* Paris, p. 71.

9. See for example, Wyn Grant (1991), *The Dairy Industry: An International Comparison*, Dartmouth Publishing Company Limited, Brookfield Vermont and Mary Marchant (1993), *Political Economic Analysis of US Dairy Policies and European Community Dairy Policy Comparisons,* Garland Publishing Inc., New York and London.

10. Derthick, M. and P.J. Quirk (1985), *The Politics of Deregulation,* Brookings Institution, Washington DC, p. 226.

11. OECD (1990), "Economy-Wide Effects of Agricultural Policies in OECD Countries: Simulation Results with WALRAS", *OECD Economic Studies,* No. 13 Winter 1989-1990, Paris

12. Unofficial estimates provided by the Canadian federal ministry: Agriculture and Agri-food Canada.

13. Kaiser, H.M. based on data from earlier published work: H.M. Kaiser (1994), ''An Analysis of Alternatives to the Dairy Price Support Program'', *Agricultural and Resource Economics Review,* No. 23, pp. 158-170.

14. Helmberger, P. and Y.H. Chen (1994), ''Economic Effects of Dairy Programs'', *Journal of Agricultural and Resource Economics,* No. 19, pp. 225-238.

15. Tauer, L.W. and H.M. Kaiser (1991), ''Optimal Dairy Policy with Bovine Somatotropin'', *Review of Agricultural Economics*, No. 13, pp. 1-17.

16. Javas, J.P., T.L. Cox and E.V. Jesse (1993), *Spatial Hedonic Pricing and Trade,* Staff Paper 367, Department of Agricultural Economics, University of Wisconsin, August.

17. Doyle, S, Ivan Roberts and Peter Connell (1995), *US Dairy Policies in 1995 US Farm Bill,* ABARE policy monograph No. 5.

18. The NZDB is required under its empowering Act to consider applications to export from other entities and must report to the New Zealand government on its administration of this role. In practice, it does license other exporters of differentiated and innovative products.

19. For a detailed analysis of the UR Agreement and Agriculture see, OECD (1995), *The Uruguay Round: A Preliminary Evaluation of the Impacts of the GATT Agreement on Agriculture in the OECD Countries,* Paris.

20. Toon Leenders, Deputy Head of Division, Milk and Dairy Products, EC DG VI, GATT Implementation: ''Short and Medium Term Perspectives'', a paper presented to the 8th Annual Conference for the European and International Dairy Industry, London, October 25-26, 1995.

21. Agra Europe (1995), (London) Ltd., *EU ©May Exceed' Non-Annex II GATT Export Limits,* September 15, E/1.

22. Agra Europe (1995), (London) Ltd., *Export Refunds Affect French Trade Surplus,* October, 27, N/4.

23. See Wilmink, H., Director, Friesland Dairy Foods and Chairman, Trade and Economic Committee, European Dairy Association, *The First Three Months: Assessing the Impact of GATT Implementation from a Dairy Industry Perspective* and Bernard Le Roy, Deputy Director, Onilait, *Analysing Policy Options for the Future of EU Dairy Subsidies: Quotas and Other Support Mechanisms,* papers presented to Agra Europe Dairy '95 Conference, London, October 25-26, 1995.

24. Schiek, W.A. (1994), 'Regional Impacts of Federal Milk Marketing Order Policy Alternatives''. *Agricultural and Resource Economics Review,* No. 23, pp. 206-217.

25. United States Department of Agriculture (1995), *1995 US Farm Bill: Guidance of the Administration,* pp. 13-15.

26. *Ontario Milk Marketing Board Annual Report, 1994.*

27. Ewing, R. (1994), ''The Canadian Dairy Industry: Institutional Structure and Demand Trends in the 1990s'', Policy Branch Working Paper 1/94, Agriculture and Agri-Food Canada, February.

28. See Fischler, F. (1995), *The Common Agricultural Policy in the 21st Century – First Thoughts,* presentation by the EU Farm Commissioner to the EU Representation in Bonn, October 9 and Agra Europe (1995), (London) Ltd., *Commission to Recommend Dairy Policy Changes,* summary of a speech by the EC Agriculture Commissioner to the International Dairy Federation Conference in Vienna, September 15, P/1.

29. *House of Commons Agriculture Select Committee inquiry into the UK Dairy Industry and CAP Dairy Regime,* Joint Memorandum by the UK Agriculture Departments, October 1995, p. 34.

30. *House of Commons Agriculture Select Committee inquiry into the UK Dairy Industry and CAP Dairy Regime,* Joint Memorandum by the UK Agriculture Departments, October 1995, p. 22.

31. European Commission (1994), ''Report on the Situation for Milk and Milk Products'', COM (94)64 final, Brussels.

32. See, for example, papers presented by Hans Wilmink, Friesland Dairy Foods, Patrick O'Neil, Avonmore Foods, John Price, UK Dairy Industry Federation, Bernard Le Roy, Onilait and Eamonn Pitts, National Food Centre of Ireland, at the Agra Europe Dairy '95 Conference, London, October 25-26, 1995.

33. Workman, R., ABN Amro Hoare Govett Ltd., *Assessing the Performance of Europe's Top Dairy Companies: Profitability, New Directions, Mergers and Acquisitions,* a paper presented to the Agra Europe Dairy '95 Conference, London, October 25-26, 1995.

34. Agra Europe (1995), (London) Ltd., *Commission to Recommend Dairy Policy Changes,* September 15, P/2.

35. Agra Europe (1995), (London) Ltd., *German Milk Summit Calls for Urgent Action,* May 26, N/1

36. OECD (1994), *Farm Employment and Economic Adjustment in OECD Countries,* Paris and OECD (1995), *Adjustment in OECD Agriculture: Issues and policy Responses,* ''A Review of Household Incomes in OECD Countries'', Paris.

37. OECD (1995), *Adjustment in OECD Agriculture: Issues and Policy Responses,* ''Assessing the Relative Transfer Efficiency of Agricultural Support Measures'', Paris.

# DAIRY POLICY AND INSTITUTIONAL ARRANGEMENTS FOR SELECTED OECD COUNTRIES

## A1.1. US dairy policy

The two main components of US dairy policy are currently the *Dairy Price Support Programme* (DPSP), and Federal (and State) *milk marketing orders.* The US dairy industry has operated under the DPSP since 1949. The DPSP is intended to stabilise dairy farmer income and lessen the seasonal instability in milk prices. This programme acts much like a buffer stock mechanism with purchases during the spring "flush production" period and releases in the "slack production" period that usually occur in the fall and winter. The DPSP operates at the wholesale-processing level of the US dairy industry rather than the farm-level due to the perishable nature of raw milk. The government supports the farm milk price indirectly by offering to buy unlimited quantities of cheese, butter, and non-fat dry milk at announced purchases prices determined by the following formula:

$$PP_i = (SP + MA_i)/(PY_i)$$

where: $PP_i$ is the purchase price for product i (i = cheese, butter, or non-fat dry milk), SP is the target-level support price for raw milk, $MA_i$ is the "make allowance" set by the government to reflect the cost of producing product i net of the cost of raw milk , and $PY_i$ is the pounds of raw milk required to make a pound of product i. If the make allowance functions as intended, manufacturers who receive the purchase price should be able to pay farmers the equivalent of the support price without losing money. However, the make allowance is not a guaranteed margin to manufacturers, nor does it guarantee that manufacturers pay farmers a price that is at least as high as the support price.

Manufacturers of butter, non-fat dry milk, and cheese sell their products to the Commodity Credit Corporation (CCC) at the determined purchase price when the wholesale market price is lower than the government set price.[1] For example, in 1992 the CCC had net purchases of 9.4 million pounds (milkfat equivalent) of butter, and 0.2 billion pounds of cheese. Recently the US dairy industry has had more of a fat surplus problem, which is reflected by the majority of government purchases being of butter rather than non-fat dry milk or cheese.

The United States also had an import quota system to accompany the DPSP. Import quotas for dairy products are authorised under Section 22 of the Agricultural Adjustment Act of 1933. Historically, import quotas have restricted dairy imports into the United States to less than 2 per cent of domestic milk production. The United States primarily imports cheese (90 per cent of all imports in 1992). Without import quotas, the DPSP could not have operated as long as world prices for manufactured dairy products are well below the US purchase prices for these products. Under the Uruguay Round Agreement, however, import quotas have been replaced by tariff-rate quotas.

In addition to direct sales from CCC supplies, dairy exports are promoted through the Dairy Export Incentive Programme (DEIP). The DEIP is an export subsidy programme which was originally directed at competition from subsidising countries (primarily the EU) in targeted markets, similar to the Export Enhancement Programme (EEP) for other US agricultural commodities. Products eligible for the DEIP are milk powders, butterfat and some cheese varieties with the highest level of DEIP bonuses paid to US exporters US$ 143 million in FY 1993.[2]

The majority of the Grade A milk produced in the United States is regulated under a system of Federal and State milk marketing orders. These orders define the rules and conditions that milk processors must follow in buying Grade A farm milk. The chief function of milk marketing orders is to implement classified pricing of milk. Farm milk sold to fluid processors is Class I milk, which receives a premium since fluid products have the most inelastic price elasticity of demand relative to all dairy products. Farm milk going into soft dairy products (*e.g.* cottage cheese, yoghurt) receives the Class II price, which is lower than the Class I price, but higher than the Class III price. Farm milk used to manufacture hard dairy products (*e.g.* butter and cheese) receives the Class III price, which is equal to the Basic Formula Price (BFP). The Basic Formula Price is an ''adjusted'' average price paid for Grade B (manufacturing grade) milk by a sample of plants in Minnesota and Wisconsin, which is the market farm price that is indirectly supported by the DPSP.

Finally, a new Class III-A price was recently introduced for non-fat dry milk, which is based on a product formula, and is usually less than the BFP. Farmers selling milk to processors regulated by a marketing order receive an average (blend) price, which is a weighted average of the class prices with the weights based on the utilisation of milk in each class. The Class II, III, and III-A prices are the same throughout the United States reflecting the fact that manufactured dairy products are bought and sold nationally. However, since fluid milk markets tend to be local or regional in scope, there is a separate Class I price for each of over 30 different federal milk order markets in the nation. Generally, Class I prices increase with the distance from Eau Claire, Wisconsin, which is the surplus area of manufacturing milk in the United States The regional nature of the Class I price is one of the most controversial features of milk marketing orders, and has contributed to regional tensions between the Upper Midwest and the rest of the United States. Milk marketing orders and the DPSP are related in that the DPSP supports the BFP, and the BFP is the Class-III price under milk marketing orders.

The Federal Agricultural Improvement and Reform (FAIR) Act agreed by the House and the Senate Conference Committee on 21 March 1996 would replace the 1990 Farm Bill and be in effect for the period 1996-2002. It would eliminate the current levy on dairy producers immediately and phase down support price for butter, milk powder and cheese over four years from US$228 per tonne in 1996 to US$218 per tonne of milk equivalent in 1999. At the end of 1999, the price support authority would be eliminated, with a recourse loan programme being implemented at US$218 per tonne of milk equivalent. The dairy Export Incentive Program would remain with the maximum volume and funding levels permitted under GATT. The Secretary of Agriculture is instructed to consolidate milk marketing orders from 33 to no more than 14 and no less than 10 in 3 years.

## A1.2. Canadian dairy policy

Under the Canadian Constitution, agriculture is a shared jurisdiction between the federal and provincial levels of government. Important to understanding the Canadian dairy system is the fact that the fluid milk market is a provincial government responsibility, while the industrial market is a federal government responsibility. This is because processed dairy products cross provincial borders and come within the federal government's jurisdiction over inter-provincial and international trade, while fluid milk does not generally cross provincial boundaries and is an nitre-provincial matter. In practice, however, this division is not clear cut, as the administration of the federal government's responsibilities for industrial milk requires the co-operation of provincial governments and marketing boards.

The federal government's jurisdiction over the industrial milk market is administered, in part, through a federal-provincial agreement known as the *National Milk Marketing Plan.* This is managed by the Canadian Milk Supply Management Committee (CMSMC), chaired by the Canadian Dairy Commission, which has producer and government representatives. There is one vote per province and a unanimity rule generally applies. Given that the milk products market in Canada is effectively saturated, the unanimity requirement for decisions by the CMSMC, and the economic importance of dairy processing to Quebec, it is difficult to make adjustments in the allocation of industrial milk quota between the provinces. The Canadian Dairy Commission is mainly responsible for the operation of dairy support programmes financed by the government and for marketing operations financed by milk producers under the provisions of the National Milk Marketing Plan.

The principal mechanisms used in the supply management system to stabilise and support prices (and thereby stabilise and increase farm incomes) are *control of domestic production and marketing; import controls* and *administered pricing.*

Production control begins with the establishment of an annual national quota, based on estimates of market needs. The principal objective is to achieve a national balance in the supply and demand for industrial milk. This is done by estimating, on a butterfat basis, the market demand for dairy products in Canada plus the volume required for its export programme, with the milk equivalent of imported dairy products being deducted, along with the volume of butterfat removed from fluid milk. This national production target or Market Sharing Quota (MSQ) is divided up among the provinces, with each province allocating its share to its producers in accordance with its own procedures.

Levies on producers to cover the costs of exporting surplus products are collected by the provincial board. Although most of the levy revenues are collected from within-quota levies, it is the over-quota levy which gives effect to supply management. It discourages producers from over-supplying their market shares because they individually pay for the surplus disposal costs involved. Industrial milk is priced to plants by classes related to end use, with returns pooled to producers.

Import quotas have limited milk and milk product imports based on quantitative restrictions. In-quota tariffs were essentially set at the Most Favoured Nation rates. The introduction of the Canada-United States Free Trade Act (CUSTA) and the North American Free Trade Act (NAFTA) had no impact on these quantities or rates. Subsequent to the Uruguay Round Agreement, import quotas have been replaced with equivalent tariff protection. The tariff-rate quotas remain the same for all products except butter (which will increase from 0 to 1 964 tonnes in 1995/96 and then in annual stages to 3 274 tonnes by 2000/01, and ice cream (which increases from 347 tonnes to 484 tonnes by 2000/01). In addition, the in-quota tariffs were reduced by 36 per cent across the board. The tariffication of import quotas required by under the UR Agreement has resulted in the introduction of initially high tariffs for dairy products (*e.g.* 237.2 per cent for skim milk powder, 351.4 per cent for butter) which are to be reduced by 15 per cent by the year 2001.

A target price for industrial milk is set annually, this being defined as "the level of return efficient milk producers would have to receive to recover their cash costs, labour and investment related to the production of industrial milk." The cost of producing milk in terms of operating costs, labour and capital costs is calculated from a sample of 350 farms in four provinces. Actual prices paid to milk shippers are determined provincially in reference to the target return, and prices generally differ among the provinces.

The federal government supports the target price for industrial milk through two programs: direct payments to milk producers, and support prices through intervention purchasing for butter and skimmed milk powder. Most of the butter purchased has been resold in the domestic market, with most of the skimmed milk powder exported. Exports of butter increased in the early 1990s as a result of increased surplus stocks, but declined significantly in 1993/94.

Fluid milk pricing is under provincial jurisdiction. Most provinces charge different prices to processors for different classes of milk depending on the end-use of the milk. All provinces charge processors a higher price for fluid milk than for industrial milk, even though the milk is identical. In 1991, the average fluid mark up above industrial was C$ 15.62/hl and the variance was C$ 10.38/hl. Fluid prices vary across provinces more than the average industrial price which in 1991 was C$ 42.80/hl with a variance of C$ 0.73/hl. The fluid mark up is determined in most provinces through a cost-of-production formula. The mark up is the difference between the Canadian Dairy Commission target price and the provincial cost of production. This price is also subject to adjustment based on negotiations between the provincial marketing board and processors. Some provinces also regulate retail fluid milk prices (*i.e.* Nova Scotia, Quebec, the Prairies).

## A1.3. New Zealand dairy policy

There is currently no direct government intervention in the NZ dairy industry with no direct income programmes, no market price supports and no import controls. The only significant role is through the legislation establishing the *New Zealand Dairy Board (NZDB)*. A brief review of the reform process is presented below.

The general economic restructuring which began in 1984 mandated the removal of all agricultural support policies. This had the greatest impact on the town milk sector of the dairy industry. The New Zealand dairy industry had been unique in that the fresh milk (*i.e.* market milk) industry was entirely separate from the manufacturing milk industry. This sector of the industry had a history of government intervention and pervasive regulation and controls going back to the enactment of the Milk Act 1944. The Act recognised the special nature of this industry and had a principal objective of ensuring the year round supply of high quality milk for New Zealand consumers at a stable price.

The primary control involved was a system of production quotas and price controls which ensured that consumers paid the higher price for this type of milk and that there were fixed prices for retail sale and household delivery. An earlier system of consumer price subsidy had been phased out in the 1970's. Since 1987, this industry has been deregulated and price controls have been gradually lifted. This deregulation and the consequent restructuring has allowed the merging of the two components of the dairy industry. Many of the fresh milk processing plants were taken over by the export co-operatives and others have become involved in processing for export. With the deregulation of the domestic market, New Zealand's dairy co-operatives compete fiercely to attract farmer suppliers and to achieve the highest payout.

Whilst the domestic market is characterised by a high degree of competition, the international marketing is still closely controlled. The origins of this control can be traced back to the Dairy Produce Export Control Act, which was passed in 1923 to establish the Dairy Control Board to act as the central export seller to counteract the power of British merchants. Most of the export dairy products are marketed through the NZDB. The Board has exclusive control over the exports either through their direct trading or through controls over firms who may wish to enter the export market. The Board has the full authority to make and carry out arrangements for acquisition and marketing of the export produce. The Board does not directly control the processing of the milk but purchases export products from the co-operatively owned processing companies. These firms are joint co-operative owners of the NZDB but compete for suppliers by attempting to minimise their processing costs.

The NZDB has been described as a multinational milk food trader and one of the world's largest farmer controlled dairy marketing organisation. The Board is the international marketing arm of the NZ dairy industry which is an integrated co-operative of manufacturing dairy companies and dairy farmers. From earning 80 per cent of its revenue from shipments of bulk butter and cheese to the United Kingdom in the late 1960's, the Board has become New Zealand's largest exporter and evolved into an international marketing co-operative with 40 subsidiary and associate companies in over 20 countries throughout the world.

More recent developments in 1995 have meant that a formal capital ownership and shareholding structure has been developed to more closely resemble a corporate structure. A proposed amendment to the Dairy Board's empowering legislation would restructure the NZDB into a co-operative marketing company owned by NZ's dairy processing co-operatives in proportion to the product they supply to it. The amendment does not propose to modify the NZDB's statutory powers but to change the dissolution provisions to ensure that the NZDB is a going concern in the event of a removal of its statutory powers. The present Dairy Board does not receive any funding from the Government and a former scheme of providing subsidised credit through the Reserve Bank was withdrawn following the economic reforms in 1984.

## A1.4.  The European Union's Common Agricultural Policy for dairy products

The United Kingdom and the Netherlands are members of the EU and as such are subject to the *Common Agriculture Policy (CAP)*. A brief review of the main policy instruments of the CAP is provided. For the purpose of this paper, however, the main interest is in the implementation of the CAP in these two countries since it is the EU dairy policy in combination with national institutional arrangements that impact on the structure and performance of the industry.

For a long period the principal price support mechanism has been the *intervention price,* calculated for the two (non-water) milk components, butter and skimmed milk powder. In the last few years, a complicated array of special measures for individual sub-sectors contributed to support domestic prices. These are welfare butter payments, subsidised sales of butter to institutions and for use in ice cream and pastry manufacture, subsidised use of skimmed milk for casein manufacture or in animal feed and discount milk for schools.

The intervention price set a floor which was maintained by intervention buying. Until 1987, intervention was an open-ended commitment, provided minimum quality standards and other specifications were met, but since March 1987, to reduce sales to intervention and to lower real price-support levels, strict limits for automatic intervention have been imposed, beyond which a tendering system operates for butter. This has reduced effective intervention prices to around 90 per cent to 95 per cent of official intervention prices. For SMP, support buying is suspended during the winter months. Butter and skimmed milk powder buying-in prices maintain their considerable margins over world prices as a result of the operation of variable levies on imports (now replaced by tariffs) and subsidies for exports. In 1992, UK prices were respectively around 100 per cent and 60 per cent higher than world fob prices.

Intervention prices are based on a target price for milk of 3.7 per cent fat content. This is the price that efficient dairies ought to be able to pay their farmers if the EU's support mechanisms are operating effectively; but it is not a price guarantee to farmers and many dairies are unable to pay the full target price. The intervention prices for butter and skimmed milk powder are derived from the target prices given standard processing ratios and production costs. Given the tendering system now in operation, the intervention milk price equivalent (*i.e.* the price that farmers should receive after allowing for processing costs) has been around 90 per cent of the target price since 1991.

It is also worth noting that although milk target prices have been set at the same ECU level in all member States, market prices in fact varied from one member State to another according to the situation and structure of the domestic market and in response to changes in domestic currency exchange rates.[3] Reforms introduced on 1 February 1995 to the EU agrimonetary system were designed to minimise these national differences.

Variable import levies have been replaced by fixed tariffs from 1 July 1995 under the Uruguay Round Agreement. These levies were designed to protect high priced dairy products within the Community from cheaper imports. Threshold (minimum support) prices were established by the Commission each year for twelve pilot products. For butter and SMP, threshold prices allowed a margin of around 12 per cent over intervention prices and the margin of protection was similar for the other pilot products. For each product, the levy was calculated as the difference between the threshold price and the most representative world market price. Variable levies for all other dairy products were derived from those for the twelve pilot products.

The introduction of *quotas* in 1984 has had a profound effect on the dairy sector, halting and indeed reversing the upward trend in production. The national quota was allocated first to dairies, then to individual farmers. If a member State exceeds its quota level, a financial penalty is passed on to over-quota dairies and ultimately to over-quota farmers. Since the penalties are triggered by national over-production, there is scope for some balancing out of under- and over-producing farmers, so individual farmers have some scope for exceeding their own individual quotas without penalty, though by how much is an unknown variable when production decisions are being made. The penalty (super-levy) is 115 per cent of the target price. Quota cannot be transferred between member States but can be bought and sold within a country if the member countries allows such transfers as is the case in the Netherlands and the UK. Table A1.1. shows the distribution of quotas among member States in 1995/96.

Table A1.1.  **European Union, milk quotas 1995/96**

|  | Delivered to dairies | Direct sales | Total sales | National shares (%) |
|---|---|---|---|---|
| Germany | 27 765 | 100 | 27 865 | 24 |
| France | 23 694 | 542 | 24 236 | 21 |
| United Kingdom | 14 270 | 320 | 14 590 | 12 |
| Netherlands | 10 982 | 93 | 11 075 | 9 |
| Italy | 9 632 | 298 | 9 930 | 8 |
| Spain | 5 222 | 345 | 5 567 | 5 |
| Ireland | 5 235 | 11 | 5 246 | 4 |
| Denmark | 4 454 | 1 | 4 455 | 4 |
| Belgium | 3 077 | 233 | 3 310 | 3 |
| Portugal | 1 836 | 37 | 1 873 | 2 |
| Greece | 626 | 5 | 631 | 1 |
| Luxembourg | 268 | 1 | 269 | |
| Austria | 2 205 | 367 | 2 572 | 2 |
| Finland | 2 342 | 10 | 2 352 | 2 |
| Sweden | 3 300 | 3 | 3 303 | 3 |
| Total | 114 909 | 2 364 | 117 273 | 100 |

*Source:*   ONILAIT (1995), *Annual report, 1995.*

## A1.5.  The UK Milk Marketing System

In the past, the major government intervention in the UK dairy industry was the *Milk Marketing Board* system established in the early 1930s and abolished in 1994. The Boards were the sole buyers of milk from producers and the sole sellers of milk for manufacturing. Under the deregulated system now in place, producers have a number of companies bidding for their milk for the first time in 60 years. One of the reasons the UK industry was chosen for review was the opportunity to examine the reasons for such a fundamental change to a well-established system and to observe the initial response of the industry to the new deregulated system.

Five Boards were established in the UK: one for England and Wales (established 1933), three for regions of Scotland (1933 and 1934) and one for Northern Ireland (1955). The rules governing their activities and their practical implementation were virtually identical. All milk producers who wanted to sell milk had to register with the Board and sell through the Board as the agency. Producers were exempt from this arrangement only if they sold most of their milk to consumers directly or, under Community legislation, if they chose to export milk if the price paid by the Board fell below a certain level. In turn, the Board was obliged to buy all of the milk which registered producers wanted to sell, provided that the milk met certain quality standards. The Boards arranged for collection of the milk and paid farmers a ''pooled price'' which reflected the weighted average return from all milk sold by the Board, adjusted for seasonal, compositional and hygiene factors and after deduction of the Board's expenses and various levies. The Board then sold the milk to dairy processors, the largest of which, Dairy Crest, was owned by the Board, at prices differentiated by use, but not by buyer.

Fundamental to an understanding of the impact of the Boards on structure and performance was the procedures by which they set prices to end-users (which depends on the use to be made of the milk) and to farmers (which depends on the milk composition and the time of year but not on the producer's location). Of these, the end-use pricing system is the most important.

The price of milk sold by the MMB was subject to negotiation by a Joint Committee comprising representatives of the Board and of the milk purchasers. Milk prices for alternative end uses were set through a formula pricing scheme which took into account the market situation for the different dairy products as well as processing and marketing costs, including an agreed return on capital and a milk/product yield factor. There were different degrees of detail in the application of the approach to different end uses but the principle was always the same. The most detailed approach, the *CATFI system (Common Approach to Financial Information)*, was applied to butter and skimmed milk powder. Under the CATFI system, information was collected on production and marketing costs, and the total costs of the final product, including depreciation and return on capital, were calculated. These are deducted from ''panel returns'' in the market, which included sales to intervention where appropriate, and the residual element converted into pence per litre of milk. If costs exceeded market returns, buyers received a rebate. If returns were higher, this was taken into account in the next price fixing round. The outcome of this system was that processors were guaranteed minimum returns.

When the UK joined the European Community, the continuation of the Milk Marketing Boards was agreed subject to two conditions. These were that: *a)* the proportion of milk produced and marketed which is consumed as whole milk or other fresh dairy products in the UK should be at least 150 per cent of the corresponding proportion for the EC as a whole when taken as an average over the previous three years and *b)* the UK should have a higher per capita consumption of milk and other fresh dairy products than the Community average. It was accepted therefore that, in due course, the Schemes would be replaced by mechanisms more in line with those in the rest of the Community. This, and concerns over the efficiency of milk marketing in the UK which stemmed from the existing system, were the major factors leading to the introduction of legislation to abolish the Milk Marketing Boards.

Although milk prices were jointly determined by the MMB and the DTF, in fact buyers paid the Board's single selling price for all raw milk and were then entitled to a rebate depending on the use made of the milk. The Board policed the system by allocating farmers to dairy companies. The liquid market had priority for supplies followed in descending order by other high valued products according to the negotiated price. If supplies were short, milk would be diverted from the low value usage (generally butter) to the closest factory producing a higher value product. If a manufacturer refused to relinquish supplies, he would forgo the "rebate", thus effectively paying a higher price than his competitors for the raw material.

The Board had, by the early 1980s, become the largest manufacturer of dairy products through its ownership of Dairy Crest, but had originally got into manufacturing solely as a result of being unable to find an alternative outlet for surplus production in the early 1930s. It began manufacturing cheese in 1934 and three years later was operating an additional nine dairies and creameries, setting up either where there were no outlets for the milk or where existing factories were in danger of going out of business. The purchase in 1979 though of the butter, SMP and cheese activities of Unigate gave Dairy Crest a dominant position in the market, with 80 per cent of the butter and 75 per cent of the SMP markets.

## A1.6.  Netherlands dairy policy

The Dutch Ministry of Agriculture (*Dutch: Ministerie van LNV*) has always been the ultimate national authority on such matters as the elaboration of policies and definition of strategies for the dairy sector. Yet, a democratisation of government policies, which started in the 1950's with the creation of the Commodity or Product Boards, led to a decentralisation of powers and competencies. To some extent, this involved greater self-regulation by the agricultural sector.

In the case of the dairy sector, the Dutch government delegated many of its tasks to the ***Dairy Product Board (Dutch: Produktschap voor Zuivel or PZ)***. The mandate of the Product Board was basically to create and perpetuate the best possible economic environment for the sustained growth of the dairy industry. The PZ was instituted in 1956 under the Industrial Organisation Act as a public-private partnership. To ensure that the interests of all those within the sector are well represented, farmers, co-operatives, private processors, employee trade unions as well as other organisations sit on the PZ's board.

As with the United Kingdom, dairy policy in the Netherlands is governed by the EU Common Agriculture Policy. The creation of the European Union (EU) and the evolution of the Common Agricultural Policy (CAP) in the 1960s came at a time when the Dutch internal markets for the basic dairy products of milk, butter and cheese were already saturated. Creation of the EU increased the potential market from the 11.4 million Dutch population to the 170 million population of the EU-6. As well, EU export refunds helped boost Dutch exports to non-EU country markets. For the Dutch dairy industry, the period since 1950 has been one of sustained growth and development of external markets.

Dutch livestock producers traditionally have used a wide range of imported non-cereal ingredients – a tendency which was reinforced by the introduction of a high-price CAP regime for cereals, plus levies on cereal-based imports. Consequently, Dutch dairy farmers have benefited from a competitive advantage over their other EU-counterparts through access to comparatively cheap feeding stuffs. Also, as a strong currency country the Dutch have benefited from the operation of the EU agrimonetary system. Under this arrangement, Dutch farmers have been protected from the full effects of an appreciating currency whilst receiving additional refunds on their exports. To date the Dutch dairy industry, and notably its marketing co-operatives, have been able to maintain their strong export position based on production efficiency and the advantages conferred by the CAP.

The Dutch dairy industry has a long standing tradition of operating via *co-operatives* (Table A1.2.). The three main co-operatives (Campina Melkunie, Friesland Dairy Foods, Coberco) control over 80 per cent of all milk supplies, giving the industry an oligopoly market structure. Dairy farmers have developed these highly organised co-operatives to perform marketing functions with considerable discriminatory power over individual producers. These co-operatives have the authority to price discriminate between members on the basis of quality standards (.in fact, low-quality producers may be expelled from the co-operative). Also, co-operatives can now decide whether or not to accept milk and/or new members according to market opportunities and the returns on investment which can be achieved. To this end, the traditional co-operative policy of free entry of members and acceptance of all milk quantities has been replaced with a more market-oriented policy. This also applies to New Zealand co-operatives.

When the Common Agricultural Policy came into effect in the early 1960s, the Dutch dairy institutional framework was reorganised in order to conform with European legislation and PZ lost some of its authority on regulations relating to agricultural policy. The Dutch government decided, however, to delegate certain of its governing functions in relation to implementation of CAP regulations to PZ. In practice, the PZ is charged with payment of export restitutions, implementation of EC quotas and super-levies on quota violations, collection of co-responsibility levies, buying and selling dairy intervention products (butter, SMP) and implementation of special regulations (*e.g.* concerning "Christmas butter", school milk, etc.).

In order to be able to carry out the above "policy" functions in the public domain, PZ receives some financing from the Dutch government. However, for its autonomous tasks such as data collection, promotion, research and inspection, expenditures are covered by the imposition of a levy, which is charged on all milk delivered to the dairies. Thus, a big part of PZ finances is derived from the dairy processing industry. The value of some of the autonomous responsibilities carried out under the auspices of by PZ are coming into question as the downstream industry becomes more market-oriented. Industry experts and government officials recognise that there are significant differences between the larger processing firms, in terms of marketing strategies, competition policy, research priorities and financial structures.

Finally, the *milk quota market* is relatively unregulated and is comparable to the transfer conditions in the UK. In the Netherlands, there is no government administrative redistribution of

Table A1.2.  **Share of co-operative firms in selected markets**

| Production | % | Exports | % |
|---|---|---|---|
| Intake of domestically produced milk | 84 | Milk and cream | 84 |
| Processed fresh milk | 86 | Skimmed milk powder | 100 |
| Cheese | 92 | Milk powder | 99 |
| Butter | 96 | Condensed milk | 96 |
| Milk powder | 69 | Butter and Butter oil | 100 |
| Condensed milk products | 90 | Cheese | 98 |

*Source:*  Produktschap voor Zuivel.

quota as is the case of most other EU countries. In France and Denmark, for example, there is a 100 per cent administrative redistribution of a quota reserve supplied from farms that cease production and, in the case of France, from a levy on land transactions. In Germany, a policy of tying quota to land has been applied. With relatively few government restrictions on the transfer of quota, generous tax provisions for the depreciation of quota expenditures and relatively high margins on milk production, quota values in the Netherlands have become among the highest in EU.

# DAIRY POLICY IMPACTS ON INDUSTRY STRUCTURE
# AND PERFORMANCE

This section examines, for each of the five countries under review, the available evidence on some of the more significant impacts of dairy policies; first, on industry structure and, second, on industry performance. Where available, empirical studies are cited to provide quantitative evidence of policy impacts. Given the large differences in terms of policy regimes, industry structure and available information, the approach to this analysis varies considerably across the countries reviewed. However, in each case an attempt has been made to examine some of the impacts on the downstream processing as well as the farm level.

## A2.1.   United States

### *Impacts on structure*

In the United States the DPSP has resulted in *excess resources allocated to milk production* and dairy product processing in the United States. The impact of the DPSP on excess milk production can be quantified by looking at net Commodity Credit Corporation (CCC) purchases on a milkfat equivalent basis since this represents the amount of milk produced in excess of commercial market needs. For example, in the decade of the 1980s, net CCC purchases of dairy products averaged 11 billion pounds per year, or 8 per cent more milk than consumers demanded (calculated from data in *US Dairy Situation and Outlook*). Because of lower support prices, CCC purchases are somewhat lower in the 1990s. Average net CCC purchases of dairy products from 1990 through 1993 were 9.2 billion pounds, which represented 6.1 per cent more milk production than was commercially demanded. Therefore, the DPSP has resulted in 6-8 per cent excess capacity in milk production since the 1980s.

The DPSP has also resulted in *excess resources in manufacturing dairy products* (not fluid products, which cannot be stored since they are highly perishable). However, the impact of the DPSP on excess production at the wholesale processing level has been different for each product (cheese, butter, and non-fat dry milk). For example, in the 1980s, the United States had significant excess production of non-fat dry milk (relative to domestic commercial needs) compared to butter and cheese. Over this decade, the CCC actually purchased over 150 per cent more non-fat dry milk than was commercially consumed. There was also substantial excess production of butter and cheese in the 1980s, with CCC net purchases, on average, representing 38.5 per cent and 10 per cent of commercial demand, respectively. In the 1990s , there is significantly less excess production of cheese and non-fat dry milk as compared to the 1980s. From 1990 through 1993, net CCC purchases of cheese were only 0.5 per cent of commercial demand, while net CCC purchases of non-fat dry milk were 42 per cent of commercial demand. The main reason for this decrease in excess production of cheese is a tremendous growth in commercial demand. The primary reason for the decrease in excess production of non-fat dry milk was the decrease in the government non-fat dry milk purchase price in this period. On the other hand, net CCC purchase of butter actually increased slightly in the 1990s, averaging 40.6 per cent of commercial demand. This occurred even though the purchase price for butter was decreased the most of all three products.

Both the DPSP and federal milk marketing orders may have had an impact on *shifting the balance of market power* in the US dairy industry. Sun, Liu, and Kaiser found that wholesale fluid milk processors tend to behave more competitively under the market equilibrium regime, implying that the DPSP has an anti-competitive influence on the market conduct of fluid processors.[4] The authors reasoned that fluid processors may behave more competitively in the market equilibrium regime because they wish to capture a larger share of the ''boom'' market, which is consistent with Rotemberg and Saloner.[5] Sun, Liu, and Kaiser found the reverse for wholesale manufactured dairy product processors, who behaved more competitively under the government supported regime. The reasoning here is that the incentive for collusive behaviour is less under the government supported regime because restricting quantity to increase price would fail since such actions would simply reduce net CCC purchases by a comparable amount, with the market price staying at the supported level. However, the statistical coefficient for this result was not statistically significantly different from zero. The study results imply that the DPSP has led to more market power on the part of wholesale fluid milk processors, but has had no significant impact on market power of wholesale manufactured processors.

Milk marketing orders impact on the *regional distribution* of dairy production and processing. The 1985 Farm Bill raised Class I milk prices in most orders relative to Class I prices in the Upper Midwest. Some regions of the country such as Texas experienced a tremendous growth in milk production since this time, and producers in the Upper Midwest attribute this growth to the increase in Class I prices in 1986. The Upper Midwest challenged the legality of this price increase in judicial court, contending that marketing orders must either be modified to allow national pooling of the higher Class I market, or eliminated. A decision on this court case was reached in 1994, where the Court ruled in favour of upholding milk marketing orders without modification. Another example of regional distortion associated with US dairy policy is that dairy manufacturers in California pay a substantially lower price for raw milk since they have higher *make allowances* (the make allowance is the cost of manufacturing a dairy product net of raw milk costs). This puts dairy manufacturers in other regions at a competitive disadvantage and has created regional tensions towards California.

*Impacts on performance*

The DPSP has resulted in *higher prices* than would otherwise result at the farm, wholesale, and retail levels of the US dairy industry. A recent study by Kaiser simulated and compared the industry-wide economic impacts of the DPSP with those under no program from 1980-90. The simulation study found, for the 1980-90 period, that the farm milk price was substantially higher (23.5 per cent on average) with the DPSP compared to a scenario with no price support program in effect. Helmberger and Chen calculated the impact of the DPSP on farm prices based on 1990 conditions. The authors found the short-run impact of eliminating the program would be a 15 per cent decrease in the farm milk price. The authors also computed a long-run impact of abolishing the program, which was defined as the steady-state solution seven years after termination of the program. The long-run impact of eliminating the DPSP was only a 3.6 per cent decrease in the farm milk price, suggesting, that after the market adjusts to deregulation, the impact on price would be significantly less than the short run impacts.

Regarding wholesale prices, the Kaiser study found that the DPSP led to substantially higher wholesale prices relative to no program. The wholesale butter price was the "most supported" under the DPSP, almost 40 per cent higher with the DPSP than without. The wholesale cheese price was 6.9 per cent higher, on average, while the wholesale fluid milk and frozen product prices were 18.2 per cent and 10.7 per cent higher, respectively. However, it is likely that the current DPSP does not have the same magnitude of impact on prices that it did for the 1980s as reported by Kaiser or by Hemlberger and Chen for 1990 due to the fact that the manufactured dairy products market is currently more competitive than it was in the 1980s because of declining purchase prices for dairy products. Consequently, elimination of the DPSP may not have as large of negative impact on prices today, as it would have had in the 1980s.

Chavas, Cox, and Jesse examined the regional impacts of milk marketing orders on farm milk price and production. At the national level, milk prices were estimated to be slightly higher due to milk marketing orders. However, the order system was found to lower prices in some regions (*e.g.* Wisconsin, Minnesota, South Dakota, North Dakota and California) and raise it in others (*e.g.* New England States, Central Region and South Atlantic) where milk prices were 3 to 6 per cent higher due to this policy. The study also quantified the impacts of milk marketing orders on wholesale prices and quantities. Milk orders had the largest positive impact on wholesale fluid milk prices, which increase by almost 10 per cent due to the policy. This increase in wholesale prices occurs because milk marketing orders raise the price of farm milk used in fluid products. On the other hand, milk marketing orders were found to have a negative impact on wholesale manufactured product prices, especially butter (−10.7 per cent) and non-fat dry milk (−9.0 per cent). By artificially raising the price of Class I milk, the cost of manufacturing milk has been lower due to more farm milk being available for Class II and III products.

US dairy policy also affects *inter-regional competition.* The DPSP has been beneficial to those regions whose plant capacity is not well aligned with changes in the commercial market place, (*e.g.* butter plants rather than cheese), those regions of the United States where milk production is growing much more rapidly than commercial markets (*e.g.* West Coast), and those regions lacking marketing organisations that could gain access to consumer markets (West Coast). The Lake States and the West Coast are the nation's surplus/reserve milk production areas. These two regions have a high degree of dependence on the DPSP as a physical outlet.

However, at the same time, the DPSP has protected other regions of the country from competition from the Lake States and West Coast by making another market available (other than their own) for these two regions. For example, the DPSP has provided an outlet for manufactured dairy products from California, which is the lowest cost region of the country in dairy manufacturing due to lower raw milk costs. This has prevented a lot of these products from moving eastward and displacing Wisconsin manufactured products, which in turn has prevented additional Wisconsin products from displacing dairy products in other regional markets. Although this was not the original intention of the DPSP, one important side-effect of this program has been to reduce inter-regional competition in US manufactured dairy products.

If the DPSP were abolished, the lowest cost regions, which also tend to be the surplus regions selling the most products to the CCC, would likely be hurt the least since they could displace current commercial sales from higher cost producers. The Chavas, Cox, and Jesse study indicate that elimination of the DPSP would affect producers in all regions of the country, but losses in producer surplus in Wisconsin and California would be lower than in all other regions. Thus, while the DPSP is beneficial to the major surplus regions of the United States, it appears to actually be more beneficial to other regions by protecting their markets from low cost manufactured products from the Lake States and Upper Midwest. However, in recent years, net CCC purchases of products (particularly cheese) have been much lower than they were in the 1980s. As a result, the impact of eliminating the DPSP on inter-regional competition would not be as severe as it would have been in the previous decade when government purchasers were higher.

US policy has also had impacts on the industry's *adaptability and market responsiveness.* One of the original intentions of milk marketing orders was to assure adequate local supplies of Grade A milk so that all regions of the country would be self sufficient in terms of fluid milk. This policy goal was meaningful back in the 1930s, when the United States did not have the technology or infrastructure to ship fluid milk long distances from surplus to deficit regions. To meet this policy goal, Class I prices were set higher in deficit (higher cost) milk areas to induce more resources into dairying and hence help make the region become self sufficient in meeting its fluid demand. Consequently, the order system stimulated growth in dairy farms in deficit-high cost regions of the country (*e.g.* Florida). The situation today is that the United States has more than enough milk from surplus regions (*e.g.* Upper Midwest) to satisfy the fluid demand of higher cost regions. Producers in the Upper Midwest, where fluid utilisation and the Class I price is the lowest, feel it is unfair that other regions of the country should receive higher Class I and blend prices because they could provide this milk at a lower cost. The Upper Midwest position is that milk marketing orders are basically trade barriers to their milk, since the system impedes the shipment of milk between orders, and the regional Class I price surface encourages excess resources into dairying.

Milk marketing orders have also contributed to excess fat production relative to commercial needs. Historically, minimum prices for milk were based on volume and fat-content under milk marketing orders. The higher the fat content, the higher the price. No premiums were paid to farmers based on other nutritional components such as protein, even though it has long been recognised that protein content and manufactured product (*e.g.* cheese) yields were positively related. At the same time, consumption of higher-fat dairy products has been steadily declining, while consumption of lower-fat products has been increasing. This has caused market inefficiencies, particularly in cheese processing. Cheese processors are disadvantaged because they have to pay the same price for raw milk with the same fat content, even if the protein contents are substantially different. Fat-based pricing of milk has also led to a fat surplus problem in the dairy industry. In response to these acknowledged problems with fat-based pricing, some milk marketing orders have changed to multiple component price policies, which price the fat and non-fat components of milk. However, the majority of milk marketing orders still utilise fat-based pricing.

## A2.2. Canada

*Impacts on structure*

Canada's supply manage system limits the *resource allocation* inefficiencies associated with high levels of price support by controlling the balance between supply and demand consistent with a desired target price for farm produced milk. This system has successfully limited surplus production to a small export sleeve aimed at ensuring adequate domestic supply given normal variations in production and consumption. However, by separating the domestic market from the international market, Canadian producers have effectively given up their ability to compete in the world market in return for a highly protected domestic market and guaranteed prices and profits. The domestic dairy market is growing at a slower rate than the rest of the agro-food sector and significantly slower than the US and world dairy markets. However, at current production costs, Canada cannot penetrate foreign markets.

One of the goals of Canadian dairy policy is the *protection of family farms.* While dairy farms remain family owned and operated enterprises for the most part, there has been significant adjustment over the past several decades and the decline in the number of dairy farms has generally been greater than for other, less-protected industries. The domestic market focus of the industry under supply management, and the relatively stable demand for milk, along with increased farm productivity have contributed to a steady decline in the number of farms and in the number of dairy cows required to meet Canadian domestic demand. The number of dairy farms fell 77 per cent from 1966 to 1986. The number of dairy farms in 1966 was nearly one-half the number of a decade earlier. Only 11 per cent of dairy farmers in 1966 were still active in 1986 and they accounted for almost half of all dairy farmers in that year.[6] Although there is a definite trend toward larger dairy farms, small and medium size family operations are the dominant structure in Canada. Dairy farming is one of the less concentrated of the major sectors in Canadian agriculture, with only 28 per cent of production realised by the largest 10 per cent of dairy farms. The high domestic price for milk, as a result of supply management, allows the minimum size for a viable dairy farm to be smaller than would otherwise be the case if prices were lower.

Similar to the US milk marketing orders, the Canadian supply management system has impacts on *regional distribution* of production and processing. The system has allowed little change in provincial market shares for milk production from when the system was originally introduced. This has inhibited structural adjustments within the Canadian dairy sector which would allow the industry to better meet changing market demands. There is little incentive for milk processors to develop new products or new markets, as the supply management system does not easily allow for the reallocation of quota rights that would be necessary for such firms to get the additional milk required to produce such products for market.

The programme benefits of Canadian dairy policies (*e.g.* high and stable incomes, high rates of return and high profitability) are capitalised into asset values which act as *a barrier to entry.* Capitalisation of programme benefits into either quota, land, or other fixed factor of production generally benefited the first generation of producers, who received quota free from the provincial marketing boards, at the expense of subsequent entrants who must purchase these assets. A study by Barichello indicated large economic rents associated with supply management policies in Canada.[7] He argues that the primary effect of these policies is to increase production rents rather than to protect smaller, high-cost operations or employment opportunities.

A National Dairy Policy Task Force Report released in 1991 agreed that high quota values have been a barrier to entry into dairy farming, making it difficult for those outside existing dairy farm families to enter the industry.[8] The need for land and specialised equipment already make the costs of entry into dairy farming high. Quotas either make entry difficult (if quota cannot be purchased) or add to the costs of entry or of expansion (if quota can be purchased). As a result of the significant rise in quota values since the inception of supply management, the capital costs and subsequent debt levels of new entrants are even higher, creating additional pressure to maintain high milk prices.

### Impacts on performance

Supply controls have contributed to both *stable and high prices* for dairy products. Dairy product prices no longer experience wide swings as a result of fluctuating supply and demand conditions. Farm prices for milk have risen gradually over the years in absolute terms but have increased substantially relative to prices of the nearest competitor, the United States. Over the

1980s, the United States reduced its support price for manufacturing milk as stocks of government purchased milk products grew to unacceptable levels. The Canada-US base price differential (Cdn Class 5 vs. US Class III) moved from virtual parity in the early 1980s to an exchange rate adjusted differential of C$ 10.22/hl by 1988, falling back to C$ 6.00/hl by mid-1989. This differential (partially masked by a weak Canadian dollar) was largely the result of a steady decline in US support prices while Canada continued to increase the base price for industrial milk was further augmented by the fact that Canadian class differentials are much larger than in the United States. Thus, for some products, such as yoghurt or ice cream, Canadian food processors have to pay up to 50 per cent more for industrial milk than their US counterparts.

The supply management system has not only stabilised but *increased dairy farm incomes* to levels that are above those of other farm types (except the supply managed poultry sector) and are well above the average for the agricultural sector as a whole, possibly suggesting excessive levels of support.. Rates of return on farm investment are also high. In a report by Jellis, the return on Canadian dairy farm assets was reported at 9.9 per cent in 1991; above both the 7.3 per cent return for all farms and above the 7.4 per cent return for US dairy farms.[9] A recent report by Brinkman *et. al.* also confirms that dairy farmers have generally fared better than farmers in non-supply managed industries.[10] The report cites evidence from the early 1970s (in the early stages of supply management before its major impact), which shows commercial dairy farms doing as well as other commercial farms, and as well as non-farm businesses with comparable resources. It also notes that, over the 1980s, while the rest of Canadian agriculture was experiencing a decline in returns, dairy farmers' returns were superior to most other farm types, although they no longer equalled non-farm sector returns.

The market protection afforded by supply management extends to the downstream industries as well. These benefits are reflected to some extent in higher *profitability for dairy processing.* On average, the profitability of the dairy processing industry compares favourably with other food processing industries, reporting the highest return on capital employed among all the food processing industries in 1987. For the same year, dairy processing exceeded all but four food industries (fruit and vegetable canneries, bakeries, other food products industries, and soft drinks manufacturing) in return on equity and in profits as a per cent of income.

Efforts to curb production may have an impact on processors by creating *overcapacity and underutilisation* of plants because there is insufficient milk to turn into manufactured products. Clearly, any quota regime that achieves a tight balance between supply and demand is going to pose problems for processing companies, particularly in seasonal troughs. In Ontario, plant supply quotas (PSQ) to allocate milk in the lowest four price classes, were originally established in 1970 based on plant throughput. At this time, almost 80 per cent of industrial milk was allocated by PSQ. By 1982/83 only 50 per cent of industrial milk went to these classes, resulting in supply shortages which were further aggravated by seasonal and yearly variations in milk supplies.

The 1991 National Dairy Task Force Report indicated that the United States has 6 times as many dairy processing plants as Canada and processes 9 times as much milk. Hence, the US system would appear to have much greater potential for capturing economies of size. However, a 1994 study, prepared for the Canadian Bureau of Competition Policy, provided evidence that suggested the structural differences between Canadian and US fluid and industrial milk processing plants may not be a major constraint to Canadian competitiveness (as opposed to the large scale differences in the poultry sector – the other supply managed sector in Canada).[11] On average, Canadian plants had slightly smaller sales and value-added and higher labour inputs (Table A2.1.). The study suggested that Canadian plants were close to being cost competitive and could compete on quality, especially in the high quality international cheese market. However, the higher raw material costs in Canada were seen as a major factor in cross-border competitiveness and trade. A number of multi-national firms indicated they could export processed dairy products if industrial milk and products

Table A2.1.  **Structure of fluid and industrial milk plant in Canada and the United States**

|  | Fluid milk plants | | Industrial milk plants | |
|---|---|---|---|---|
|  | Canada | US | Canada | US |
| Number plants | 159 | 964 | 221 | 1 431 |
| Production workers/plant | 39.3 | 37.3 | 37.8 | 33.9 |
| Admin. and mngt. workers/plant | 44.4 | 38.1 | 17.8 | 12.5 |
| Sales/plant (C$ mn) | 24.7 | 29.9 | n.a. | n.a. |
| Value-added/plant (C$ mn) | 5.6 | 7.6 | 5.0 | 5.8 |

n.a.: not available.
*Source:* George Morris Centre (1993), *Profile of Canada's Food Processing Industry*, Guelph, Ontario.

(*e.g.* pizza cheese) used in further value-added products were made available in Canada at competitive prices.

The supply management system has also restricted industry *adaptability and competitiveness*. While the National Milk Marketing Plan provides for movement of quota between provinces, there has been no significant increase in domestic requirements which would require new quota to be allocated, and very little reallocation of existing quota across provincial boundaries has yet been achieved. The result is an allocation of production that doesn't fully reflect provincial comparative advantage nor fully respond to changes in provincial population patterns and market opportunities. Hence, both farm production and processing costs are higher than they might otherwise be.

The 1991 National Dairy Policy Task Force Report, comparing the Canadian and US dairy industries, found that Canadian producer competitiveness was negatively affected by smaller herd size, lower cow productivity, and higher debt load. To capture economies of scale in milk production, the minimum viable sized dairy farm is estimated to be 100-150 cows. The average herd size of commercial milk producers in Ontario and Quebec is presently 41-43 cows. A number of studies, cited by Jelliss, have confirmed that Canadian milk production costs are noticeably above those of the United States and the Netherlands, more than double those of Ireland and more than three times those of low-cost producers such as New Zealand. The National Task Force Report also found that Canadian processor competitiveness was reduced by a lower rate of plant rationalisation (*i.e.* smaller size), a lower level of plant utilisation, and lower labour productivity.

## A2.3.  New Zealand

### Impacts on structure

Although the overall domestic and international welfare impacts of the NZDB exclusive control over exports may be small, there are clear impacts on the structure of the existing industry and the behaviour of individual firms. There are no restrictions on overseas firms processing NZ milk in New Zealand but they do require a licence from NZDB to export dairy products. The current legislation places restrictions on domestic and overseas firms becoming involved in export

71

marketing of New Zealand milk products. Any change in legislation would have some impact on the activities of such firms.

Co-operatives play a major role in *marketing and processing* in New Zealand. They are registered under the Co-operative Dairy Companies Act and only shareholders supplying milk may vote or stand for election to a Company Board of Directors. Shares are allocated in proportion to the quantity of milkfat supplied, and the company may require any shareholder, who has not supplied milk or cream in the preceding 12 months, to sell back his/her shares to the Company. In this manner, only active suppliers of milk take a full part in running the co-operative. The co-operative dairy companies are independent commercial entities and they have full power to make their own manufacturing decisions. The NZDB, which is also controlled and operated by the dairy farmers through their co-operatives, buys and sells all the export production of these dairy co-operative companies. The dairy board purchases products for export from the co-operatives and is responsible for the transportation and export marketing of the products in international markets. This activity is supported by an extensive network of international subsidiary firms, both partly and wholly owned by the Board. The major policy issues are hinged on the role of the NZDB as a single seller of export products.

Although the NZDB has often been described as a monopoly, in fact it is only a *monopoly exporter* often described as a single selling agent. The Board does not have any direct control on the total production of dairy products. Whilst the Board cannot capture true monopoly profits it has control on marketing destination, product mix and nature of the promotional activities. Zwart states that in economic terms the Board is unable to capture any pure monopolist profits, but can increase farmer returns through price discrimination in export markets which ensures that high priced markets are not flooded, and that markets are developed in an orderly manner.[12] With its responsibility as a sole exporter of NZ dairy products (granted under the Dairy Board Act, 1961), the Board has managed to penetrate the 5 per cent of what has been described as a highly regulated and distorted world dairy market.

The Board does have the characteristics of a *monopsonistic buyer* of dairy products. Because the board has exclusive access to dairy products for export and because the overwhelming majority of product is exported, it would be possible for the organisation to reduce the price to growers and cause a reduction in production which would maximise returns to the Board. This is unlikely to happen because the Board is owned by the producers themselves, but it does suggest that it is difficult to provide a benchmark against which the farm price can be compared. Concerns about local monopsonistic power have led to the development of strong producer-owned co-operatives in dairy industries around the world.

The structural implications of the NZDB marketing strategies are difficult to assess. In a competitive industry, firms would normally choose their own size and structure through very extensive monitoring of the business environment and the development of appropriate strategies for particular markets. This would result in a wide range of distribution channel structures and variable-sized businesses that pursue independent strategies. General management theory would not assume that complete control over a distribution channel is appropriate or advantageous. Schroder, Wallace and Malvondo note that the internal structure and marketing activities of the New Zealand Dairy Board would appear to reflect many of these realities.[13] The Board has made substantial investments in the distribution channel and trades in a wide range of products.

While this structure may emulate that of a multinational agribusiness firm, the constraints which may be imposed by the exclusive nature of the Board are not obvious. From a management perspective, flexibility and choice of distribution channel are seen to be important in the development of appropriate strategies for each firm. However, with *producer ownership,* the opportunity for individual firms to use complex contractual arrangements to spread the risks associated with investment in the distribution system is constrained. Under highly controlled marketing systems farmers may be placed in a position of making investments or owning assets in order to control the distribution channel which may be less than optimal.

### Impacts on performance

The lack of domestic intervention means that the NZDB has only an impact on the domestic market for dairy products to the extent that most of the production is exported, and the lack of government funding means that there are no impacts on taxpayers. This has meant that the main issue is ability of the Board to *increase exports and returns* to producers in the dairy industry. Several studies have described the economic arguments which show that from a theoretical point of view there are potential gains from the centralised control of exports in a market.[14] The theory of price discrimination shows that equating marginal revenues rather than prices across market segments can lead to higher average returns. Because total production is not controlled, these benefits are not monopoly rents, but rely on influencing market allocation and product mix decisions within the industry. The most obvious examples would involve discriminating between alternative export markets and between different product mixes.

To the extent that the NZDB can influence the product mix in the processing sector it would be possible to extract *economic rents* from the differing elasticities of demand in the alternative product markets. In a market with competitive exporters the economic rents associated with such activities would be eroded by arbitrage between the exporters. In a report on agricultural marketing, Hussey suggested that such benefits are likely to be small except for the obvious cases such as capturing the rent from voluntary quotas. While an empirical debate about the size of such benefits may continue, it is clear that some potential aggregate benefits do exist and could be captured by a single selling marketing board.

The recent report by Hussey provides probably the most comprehensive and public review of agricultural marketing that has been available in New Zealand for some years.[15] The report also includes criticism of producer boards based on the *pooling of returns* from price discrimination. More generally, it argues that where returns differ in particular markets there will be over-production and the maximum benefits to producers will not be captured from the market place because prices to producers are pooled and the real marginal returns to additional production are masked. This potential problem is caused by aggregating returns from diverse activities and having a marginal revenue in the aggregate market which is less than the prices paid to farmers.[16] A more general analysis would suggest that in terms of producer returns, single selling and price pooling is superior to competitive markets, but not as profitable as price discrimination with production control. This point has not been lost in the industry concerned, and is reflected in policies such as moratoriums on dairy production and charges for new entrants to the industry, all of which have been the topic of debate in New Zealand.

Hussey argues that another form of pooling comes from including returns from other products and capital investments in farm prices. This is certainly the case with the NZDB but it is also an equivalent problem in almost all co-operative firms. The fact that co-operatives have complicated capital structures which often make it difficult to separate product returns from capital returns is of concern to economists and financial analysts. Certainly, their prevalence in agriculture markets around the world and their ability to compete with firms with more conventional capital structures cannot be ignored.

Producer controlled marketing boards which have extensive control over the marketing of products are often seen to be lacking in *innovation*. This is a potential problem with the NZDB where it has been argued that smaller more competitive firms are more likely to actively seek innovation in product and market development. There have been cases cited which suggest that some opportunities are not actively pursued, but there is also evidence that larger organisations of this type are more likely to allocate funds to research and development which will have benefits to producers. These are common economic arguments but there does not appear to any clear evidence to support either view in this situation. The current policy of allowing other firms to export approved products would seem to go some way to meeting concerns in this area and the government has recently moved to make this process more effective.

The NZDB has the potential to act as a *price discriminating* firm on international markets and thus capture any benefits from price differences which may exist across markets. While this can be viewed as a possible source of distortion in international markets, Hussey suggested that given the low level of producer benefits, these impacts are likely to be small. The level of competition for bulk dairy products in international markets, and the relative size of exports in relation to domestic production, would mean that there are few opportunities to use simple market power as a source of price discrimination. The major form of discrimination is likely to be from changing product mix and developing branded products which capture the opportunities for "New Zealand" dairy products. In fact, reducing the production of products which have an inelastic demand could theoretically assist other countries by maintaining those prices. This could have benefits for the producers in all countries and is quite different from simple price discrimination.

## A2.4.  United Kingdom

*Impacts on structure*

EU membership in 1973 and access to the CAP raised the price of milk used in processing and the pool price paid to farmers, which provoked a *supply response.* As output increased, the total quantity of milk going to the liquid market rose while its share fell and the share into processing increased. Although the demand for cream, yoghurt, etc., was growing at a steady rate, this was not sufficient to take up the expansion in production and the "surplus" found its way into the intervention products, resulting in expansion in processing and storage capacity. Intervention stocks overflowed and this story was repeated throughout the Community. Action was needed and the introduction of quotas was the response.

Table A2.2. shows the steady *reduction in production* that quotas have induced in the UK over the last decade. Quotas were originally fixed at 1981 milk production plus 1 per cent. An initial over response by many UK milk producers resulted in production in the first year being 232 mn litres (1.5 per cent) under quota. Within two years of the quota regime being introduced, the system ran into difficulties because the super-levy system was not a sufficient deterrent against producers exceeding their individual quota and penalties significantly increased. Production has since remained fairly close to annual quota, which has been progressively cut back, with UK milk sales declining by about 18 per cent over the 1984-94 period. Quota reductions have had an obvious impact on the milk processing sectors, particularly butter and skimmed milk powder. Together with tighter intervention conditions, quotas have reduced supplies and created excess processing capacity.

The operation of quotas within the EU has had the effect of locking-in the *location of milk production* by country that existed in 1984. Production cannot respond to changes in costs, technology (*e.g.* of transportation, which may enable trade where none previously existed) or demand. However, provisions exist in the EU regulations for quotas to be tradable within member

74

Table A2.2.  **UK milk production**

| | Production (m. litres) | Compared with quota | |
|---|---|---|---|
| | | +/– m. litres | % |
| 1983/84 | 16 435 | – | – |
| 1984/85 | 15 240 | –232 | –1.52 |
| 1985/86 | 15 289 | +8 | 0.05 |
| 1986/87 | 15 363 | +96 | 0.62 |
| 1987/88 | 14 448 | +56 | 0.39 |
| 1988/89 | 14 023 | +78 | 0.56 |
| 1989/90 | 14 133 | n.a. | n.a. |
| 1990/91 | 13 969 | +35 | 0.25 |
| 1991/92 | 13 628 | +15 | 0.11 |
| 1992/93 | 13 440 | –11 | –0.08 |
| 1993/94 | 13 570 | +100[1] | 0.74 |

n.a.: not available.
1.   Provisional.
*Source:*   Milk Marketing Board, EC *Dairy Facts and Figures*, UK.

States. In practice, quota movements mainly result from administrative transfers and there is little private trading of quota except in the UK and the Netherlands.

Since it is unlikely that it will be profitable to import large quantities of liquid milk from outside the United Kingdom for processing,[17] quotas also have the effect of determining the **scale of manufacturing** activity. They do not, however, determine the product mix of the manufacturing activity, nor the ownership of the companies. Wilson, Traill and Strak provide evidence to suggest that the UK milk marketing system, operating with the existence of quotas, has developed a milk processing industry that can only compete in the production of low value manufactured products.[18] The high-value and dynamic components of the sector rely to a large extent on imports or manufacturing activity in the UK by foreign owned companies. The latter may not be especially harmful to the UK dairy farming sector, but may reflect ownership advantages which foreign firms have developed through the institutional environment existing in their home countries, allowing them to grow and expand abroad, while the UK institutional environment has not favoured innovative activity by UK firms.

The introduction of quotas in 1984 interrupted a steady increase in **average milk yield** per cow, as can be seen in Table A2.3. Many farmers opted for less intensive production systems, with overall output 'capped' by quotas while less intensive farmers kept on intensifying their operations. With farmers now able to expand again, mainly via quota buying and leasing, the average cow yield increase has resumed, and average herd yields reached record levels last year, and appear still to be rising.

### Impacts on performance

Quotas have caused a sharp cut-back in milk production and the UK butter processing , as the main residual market, and to a lesser extent the SMP processing, were the destination most affected by the cut-backs. The capacity built-up during the period of expansion became **excess processing**

Table A2.3.  **Milk yields in the UK**

Kg per cow

| | England and Wales | Scotland | Northern Ireland | United Kingdom |
|---|---|---|---|---|
| 1974/75 | 4 070 | 4 045 | 3 795 | 4 500 |
| 1979/80 | 4 715 | 4 535 | 4 325 | 4 670 |
| 1982/83 | 5 085 | 4 990 | 4 830 | 5 055 |
| 1983/84 | 4 950 | 4 970 | 4 850 | 4 940 |
| 1984/85 | 4 765 | 4 860 | 4 575 | 4 770 |
| 1985/86 | 4 930 | 4 865 | 4 600 | 4 880 |
| 1986/87 | 4 985 | 5 005 | 4 550 | 4 945 |
| 1987/88 | 4 870 | 4 990 | 4 635 | 4 870 |
| 1988/89 | 4 915 | 5 030 | 4 585 | 4 895 |
| 1989/90 | 5 070 | 5 095 | 4 840 | 5 050 |
| 1990/91 | 5 115 | 5 130 | 4 760 | 5 080 |
| 1991/92 | 5 175 | 5 135 | 4 825 | 5 135 |
| 1992/93 [1] | 5 220 | 5 160 | 4 840 | 5 175 |

1.   Provisional.
*Source:*   Milk Marketing Board, EC *Dairy Facts and Figures*, UK.

*capacity.* A more market-based system would respond to this new situation by rationalising or closing factories, but in the UK, the CATFI formula pricing system came into play. Since the price set for milk used to make butter was based on the costs of production, excess capacity simply meant a higher average cost and therefore a lower price paid for the raw product, milk. The burden was passed back to farmers and there was no incentive for processors, whose profits were assured, to adjust to the new situation. Eventually, the MMB decided that it would be cheaper to pay companies to shut down factories to reduce excess capacity, but this was also expensive and it was farmers, through the milk pool price, who assumed the additional costs. The result was that despite the existence of a monopoly marketing board whose objective was to raise farmers' returns, farmers in the UK were receiving less for their milk than virtually all other European farmers, as demonstrated in Table A2.4.

The impact of interventions in the industry on *wholesale and consumer prices* has changed over time. The MMB was not a true monopolist because it could not control the quantity of production, so the option of reducing supplies to both liquid *and* manufactured markets to drive up prices in both did not exist. Competition from imports (or potential imports) controlled the Boards' selling prices. Until the UK joined the EC in 1973, imports from Commonwealth countries were free of duty so, although the UK never quite met the conditions to be considered a "small country" in economic terms, manufactured milk prices were effectively determined on world markets. The liquid milk market had also been controlled with government setting maximum retail prices. This effectively placed a ceiling on producers returns from liquid milk. It was not until the end of 1984 that these controls were finally abolished.

During the transition period and following full EU membership, the manufactured milk price was raised and a floor established by the butter and skimmed milk powder (SMP) intervention prices. Prices at which manufacturers sold other dairy products (*e.g.* cream, yoghurt, etc.) to retailers, which are the crucial prices that determine Board selling prices under the regulated pricing system (as discussed in Section I of this annex), were set, taking into account competition from

Table A2.4.   **EU milk producer prices**

ECU/100 kgs

|  | 1987 | 1988 | 1989 | 1990 | 1991 | 1992 |
|---|---|---|---|---|---|---|
| Germany (West) | 24.58 | 26.47 | 28.65 | 26.43 | 25.42 | 25.71 |
| France | 23.44 | 23.81 | 24.72 | 24.09 | 23.24 | 23.62 |
| Italy | 32.85 | 33.00 | 34.53 | 34.48 | 33.72 | 33.47 |
| Netherlands | 24.88 | 26.72 | 27.85 | 25.21 | 25.40 | 26.03 |
| Belgium | 23.16 | 24.45 | 26.22 | 22.82 | 22.26 | 22.76 |
| Luxembourg | 25.23 | 26.04 | 29.10 | 29.21 | 26.11 | 25.13 |
| United Kingdom | 23.49 | 24.55 | 25.05 | 23.95 | 23.41 | 23.72 |
| Irish Republic | 21.50 | 23.61 | 26.06 | 22.46 | 21.30 | 22.54 |
| Denmark | 26.01 | 28.25 | 29.26 | 28.27 | 27.70 | 27.12 |

*Source:*   Milk Marketing Board, *EC Dairy Facts and Figures 1993.*

imports. Traditionally, imports have been most costly for liquid milk and least costly for processed products, particularly butter for which the UK negotiated special import quotas for NZ. For all products of course, variable import levies were applied. The outcome was that the wholesale price for processed dairy products has been close to the floor established by the intervention prices of butter and SMP.

The regulation in the milk sector resulted in wide differentials between the prices of milk for the liquid market and for manufacture. These stemmed from the high cost of importing fresh milk, the large imports of processed products at world or minimum import prices and the differentiated monopoly operated by the MMBs. Some 30 years ago the differential was as much as 400 per cent although, for much of the last decade, the liquid milk premium was around 50 per cent. In the months just before the abolition of the MMBs, the differential narrowed sharply. This was in part in anticipation of deregulation but also because of devaluation which raised the prices of manufactured milk product, of some resistance by consumers to higher liquid milk prices and of increased competition to doorstep delivery from supermarkets. Under the new marketing system, the price differentials will reflect only the quality, composition and continuity of milk supply.

Traill and Henson examined the incidence of price transmission under imperfect competition in the UK yellow fats market (*e.g.* butter, margarine and low-fat dairy spreads).[19] They sought to determine whether the butter intervention price, which effectively establishes a floor wholesale price, in fact affects the retail price of margarine which is not supported under the CAP. Empirical results indicated that the price of butter influenced the price of margarine, implying that the impact of the CAP dairy regime would cause **consumer surplus losses** outside the dairy sector.

A major problem for the UK milk processing industry has been the **seasonal variation** in milk production, from a peak supply in May to a trough in August or September (November in Scotland and Northern Ireland). The operation of pricing milk by formula has meant that there has been no incentive for processors to make their operations more seasonally efficient because if they remain "inefficient" (*i.e.* their costs remain high, dairy farmers have to pay the price of inefficiency via lower manufacturing milk prices. This has meant that for many years the Boards, especially the MMB for England and Wales (E&W) have made every effort to iron out seasonal variations in milk supply.

In the late 1980s the MMB (E&W) substantially increased the incentives and penalties to persuade producers to change calving patterns to improve the seasonal balance of milk supply. The scheme worked well and by 1993 May milk production was only 5 per cent more than in the trough month compared to 50 per cent in 1987. However, presumably judging that such a wide spread of seasonal prices would leave it vulnerable in the "free market" after deregulation of the Boards, the MMB announced that from April 1994 (when the statutory milk boards were due to end) the summer incentive would be halved.

A market system would establish price differentials such that the extra cost of producing milk out of season would be equal to the extra cost of processors buying milk at low cost summer prices and storing the milk in the form of butter and cheese for consumption in the winter. As well as direct storage costs, the processors would have to pay for the extra capacity needed to process all at one time of year rather than spread evenly throughout the year. This could be quite considerable and it may be that the Board's approach was near optimal.

UK dairy policy has also had an impact on the **spatial pricing** of dairy products. In recent years, the Scottish MMBs have invariably paid the highest price to producers, primarily because virtually no butter is made in Scotland and butter is usually the lowest-earning end product. Northern Ireland has paid the lowest price, mainly because only about 17 per cent of milk in Northern Ireland goes into the higher priced liquid milk market. However the difference between the payouts narrowed substantially in 1992/93, with the Scottish "premium" dropping to 2 per cent and the Northern Ireland "discount" dropping to 3 per cent. In the latter case, a contributing factor might have been the growing element of competition in Northern Ireland, with Strathroy Milk Marketing (accounting for nearly 10 per cent of all milk in the province) paying slightly higher prices than the Northern Ireland MMB in 1992/93.

In contrast, producer prices have not varied at all within a Board region. The payment of a single pooled price to producers for milk across each Board denies the principles of specialisation in production according to competitive advantage which should be reflected in spatial and temporal price differences. Those farmers located close to a major urban centre or to a manufactured milk plant have received the same price for their milk as those with no location advantages. This system has promoted an inefficient spatial distribution of milk production (*i.e.* one which minimises direct production costs for any given output but does not minimise the sum of production and transportation costs). Peripheral regions have received favoured treatment.

Finally, there is some evidence that **competition and rivalry** have been limited both by the CAP arrangements and the operation of the UK milk marketing system, which have protected small firms, enabled the survival of manufacturers whose basic aim was to produce bulk products, and shielded those manufacturers from price competition through the formula pricing system. Of course, the overall size of the UK dairy industry is constrained by milk quotas. The issue, however, is whether the UK industry is developing/maintaining a value-added processing industry or is focusing on low value production with value-added processing carried out by foreign firms based in the UK. There is some evidence to suggest UK performance has been weak in this regard according to Wilson, Traill and Strak, who document the major inroads made by foreign-owned firms into the UK dairy industry, particularly at the high-value end of the market. This is in contrast to much of the rest of the agro-food industry, where domestic firms perform well and are a dominant force throughout Europe (and beyond), particularly in processed food markets.

## A2.5.  The Netherlands

*Impacts on structure*

Structural adjustment at the farm level was significantly affected by the introduction of the CAP dairy quotas and super levy system in 1984. Over the 1975-83 period and prior to the introduction of quotas, the **number of farms** had been declining by 4.2 per cent (about 3 800 farms) per year on average while the number of dairy cows was increasing by 1.7 per cent per year (Table A2.5.). The average dairy herd increased from 24 to 41 cows and average milk output per farm increased by over 90 per cent. After the introduction of the quota system, the decline in the number of dairy farms continued at an average annual rate of 3.4 per cent (1983-93 period) but the number of milk cows also decreased by 3.1 per cent per year and the average dairy herd size remained relatively stable. As a result, Dutch milk production in 1993 was 16 per cent lower than in 1983 although the average production per farm still increased 26 per cent.

Originally, Dutch dairy farmers were strongly opposed to the implementation of quotas but have since become supporters because of reasonable incomes, stable prices and additional revenue (windfall gains) provided by the sale or lease of quotas. At the margin, the most efficient farmers have been willing to pay over one-half the farm gate price of milk (*e.g.* Gld 0.40 for a single kg of milk priced at Gld 0.77) for leasing production rights. (Current lease price for milk quota is about one-tenth the quota selling price). Prices for the transfer of permanent production rights have been recorded as high as Gld 5.00 per kg. Limited restrictions on **quota transfers** and the more recent opportunity to lease quotas, have resulted in a large traded volume. Over the period 1984-1988, the annual volume of quotas traded increased from 50 000 tonnes to 300 000 tonnes. When leasing was introduced in 1989 this traded volume fell to 180 000 tonnes, while the volume of lease contracts more than doubled in just two years from 124 000 tonnes to 297 000 tonnes in 1991. In 1992/93, 400 000 tonnes of milk were produced under lease contract, with about 30 per cent of dairy farmers involved in leasing or trading quotas.

The current system of tradable quotas may provide an optimal allocation of production rights as the most efficient farmers with high margins should be best able to bid for available quota. However, it also means that *young entrants* to the industry have to find additional capital either to

Table A2.5.  **Structural adjustment in milk production in the Netherlands**

|  | 1975 | 1983 | 1993 | Average annual % change 1975/83 | Average annual % change 1983/93 |
|---|---|---|---|---|---|
| Milk cows (1 000) | 2 218 | 2 526 | 1 747 | +1.7 | −3.1 |
| Milk production (1 000 kg) | 10 286 | 13 207 | 11 030 | +3.5 | −1.6 |
| Number of dairy farms | 91 560 | 61 148 | 40 525 | −4.2 | −3.4 |
| Dairy herd/farm | 24.2 | 41.3 | 43.1 | +8.8 | +0.4 |
| Production/farm (kg) | 112 341 | 215 984 | 272 178 | +11.5 | +2.6 |
| Yield/cow (kg) | 4 637 | 5 228 | 6 315 | +1.6 | +2.1 |

*Source:*  Landbouw Economisch Institut and Centraal Bureau voor de Statistiek, 1984, 1993, 1994.

buy out other family interests (raising the problem of whether to use average or marginal quota values) or to acquire extra quota. Further, farmers in support of the system fail to take account of the fact that the higher values ascribed to milk quota generally imply lower values for other fixed assets such as land.

The dairy processing sector expanded rapidly along with increased production, stimulated by support under the EU CAP. In the mid-1980s, when quotas were introduced, problems of **surplus capacity** soon emerged. At first, dairy firms tried to address this problem by competing aggressively to acquire milk. Despite large intervention stocks overhanging the market at that time, milk prices were bid up as if it were in short supply (which in turn resulted in a bidding up of quota values as farmers sought to increase market access). Co-operatives, in an attempt to avoid closing additional plants, tried to import milk supplies with varying degrees of success. While some private processing firms also followed this policy, they generally moved much more quickly to rationalise capacity via plant closures.

From 221 dairy firms in 1981, less than one-fifth (28 firms) remained in 1994, of which 6 firms only collect milk with no processing activities (Table A2.6.). The number of processing dairy firms declined by over 73 per cent over the twelve-year period 1981-1993. Thirteen of the remaining processing firms are co-operatives. In the case of large multinationals, such as Nestlé, some processing was redirected to areas where raw milk prices were lower.

By the early 1990s, the **co-operatives** realised that their strategy was unsustainable and that capacity had to be reduced. This change of policy has begun to redress the market balance while farmer members have lost some of their price advantage. However, the dairy processing sector as a whole remains heavily dependent upon export restitutions and will be significantly affected if these restitutions are curtailed.

### Impacts on performance

Due to CAP-supported milk prices and relatively high operating margins, large **economic rents** associated with production rights have been captured in quota values. Rising quota values imply higher fixed costs (if quota is purchased as a permanent asset) or higher variable costs (through short-term lease arrangements) and, therefore, a reduction in the competitive advantage of Dutch dairy farmers. The support of milk prices no doubt allows some smaller, less efficient producers to remain in the sector while creating a barrier to entry for new farmers.

High quota values, however, have provided the incentive and the financial means for many low margin producers, and those with no successor, to leave farming by selling or leasing their quota to more efficient, expanding producers. At the current market price for quota of Gld 4.5 per kg, the quota for an average dairy farm producing 275 000 kg of milk would be worth over

Table A2.6.   **Structural adjustment in the dairy industry in the Netherlands**

|  | 1981 | 1984 | 1987 | 1990 | 1994 |
|---|---|---|---|---|---|
| Number of dairy firms | 221 | 153 | 138 | 55 | 28 |
| Number of dairy processors | 84 | 57 | 46 | 30 | 22 |

*Source:*   Produktschap voor Zuivel, 1993, 1994.

Gld 1.2 million. In this manner, the system of liberal quota transfers in the Netherlands has, to some extent, stimulated structural adjustment. Accumulation of milk quota has taken place especially among farms with more than 200 000 kg of milk (approximately 30 cows), generally expanding by around 20 per cent in quota terms.

It has been the intensive dairy operations (with the highest margins) which have acquired quota in recent years and become even more intensive. About half of all dairy farms are considered extensive operations by Dutch standards (less than 10 000 kg of milk per hectare). Less than 7 per cent of this group acquired quota during the 1988-91 period despite the attractive economies of size while 17 per cent sold off some or all of their quota.

This structural adjustment is at odds with *agri-environment policy* which tends to discourage highly intensive farming. The Netherlands is the most densely populated country in Europe and agriculture exerts severe pressures on the environment. Current government agri-environmental regulations are designed to encourage less intensive farming by stipulating the maximum use of minerals per hectare. However, extensive operations may have difficulty competing with the more intensive operations for available quota.

The Agricultural Economics Research Institute in the Netherlands analysed the effects of quota regulations for the competitive position of dairy farmers. Over the 1983-94 period, the number of dairy cows decreased by 30 per cent and as a result the price for roughage feeds and the quantities purchased decreased. A similar effect was observed for concentrate feeds. Fixed costs, however, increased. Fixed costs per kg of milk, compared with a milk price of about 80 cents, rose as follows: land and buildings by 7 cents, labour by 5 cents, machinery by 3.5 cents, other costs by 7 cents, of which costs for buying and leasing quota was by 5 cents.

During the three decades prior to the imposition of milk quotas, dairy processing firms operated in a non market oriented environment and many focused on operational efficiency in response to intervention buying under the CAP by supplying basic products to minimum standards and concentrating on operational and administrative efficiencies. As such, these dairy firms had little market orientation – in fact they often had no marketing or product development activities. Large quantities of a few standard products were sold into the internal and export markets. Processing efficiency and generic product quality (*e.g.* fat and protein content of milk, computerised dairy processing systems, feed conversion ratios) showed steady development but there was little development of new products and markets. In response to the expansion of the EU, and supported by the rapid expansion in milk supplies, firms increased capacity by closing old plants and investing in much larger processing units to gain economies of scale.

The introduction of the milk quota system in 1984 was a big shock to the dairy processing industry. Production being constrained, excess supply was reduced and the share of dairy products in EU total agricultural support decreased significantly (from 30 per cent in 1984 to 13 per cent in 1994). Besides, economic growth could no longer be achieved through expanding volumes of milk deliveries with more investment in product and market innovation necessary. Some of the greatest changes have occurred within the co-operative organisations which are becoming more market-oriented and seeking greater forward integration while farmer-members see themselves more as investors in their co-operative business. New financial structures mean that farmers may invest in their co-operatives beyond the level necessary to maintain capital investment on a parity with milk supplies. The result is, to some degree, a decoupling of milk supplies and investment. The large co-operative Friesland Dairy Foods, for example, has foregone its role as a price leader in order to pay a dividend separately on the shares held by members.

There are clear differences discernible between the *marketing strategies* by the big three co-operatives in terms of product and market focus (*e.g.* one now focuses on the liquid milk market and special dairy-based industrial products, others on cheese or condensed milk production). From an institutional point of view, the consequence of this increased market orientation (and increased concentration of dairy processing) has been a gradual reduction in power and functions of established regulatory bodies in favour of a strengthening of the independent position of the big dairy co-operatives. The interests represented by each of the three main dairy co-operatives have become so wide in scope and so different between themselves that public administration is less appropriate that it was in the last decade.

# Notes and references

1. The CCC also sells product back to the market whenever the wholesale market price is higher than 110 per cent of the purchase price. Thus, the DPSP also acts to prevent prices from rising above specified levels.

2. Blayney, Don P., James J. Miller and Richard P. Stillman (1995), *Dairy: Background for 1995 Farm Legislation,* (AER-705), USDA Economic Research Service, Washington, DC.

3. For a discussion of the EU agrimonetary system, see Gerard van Balsfoort, Netherlands Ministry of Agriculture, *Agrimonetary Policy and the Dairy Industry,* a paper presented at the Agra Europe Dairy '95 Conference, London, October 25-26, 1995.

4. Sun, C.H., D.J. Liu, and H.M. Kaiser (1994), "Estimating the Market Conduct of Manufactured and Fluid Processors using a Switching Regime Framework: The Case of the US Dairy Industry". Submitted to the *Journal of Agricultural and Resource Economics,* October. This recent study by Sun, Liu, and Kaiser looked at the role of the DPSP in influencing the conduct of wholesale fluid and manufactured dairy product processors. The authors argued that the DPSP causes prices to be determined under two different structural regimes: a "market equilibrium" regime, which occurs when the market price is above the support price, and a "government supported" regime, which occurs when the support price is the effective price. Based on an imperfect competition model that used an econometric framework that accounted for the switching market regimes, the authors examined whether the DPSP had a pro- or anti-competitive influence on the conduct of wholesale processors.

5. Rotemberg, J.J. and G. Saloner (1986), "A Supreme-Theoretic Model of Price Wars During Boom Periods", *American Economic Review,* 76, pp. 390-407.

6. Moloney, D. (1990), *Structural Change in Canada's Dairy and Poultry Farm Sector: 1966-86,* a paper prepared for the Economic Studies and Policy Analysis Division, Agriculture Canada, June.

7. Barichello, Richard R. (1991),"Capitalizing Government Program Benefits: Evidence of the Risk Associated with Holding Farm Quotas", unpublished mimeograph.

8. *Evolution of the Canadian Dairy Industry,* a report of the National Task Force on Dairy Policy submitted to the federal Minister of Agriculture, Ottawa, May 31, 1991.

9. Jellis, Arvin D. (1995), *Competitiveness Assessment of the Canadian Dairy Products Industry,* Policy Branch draft working paper, Agriculture and Agro-food Canada, January.

10. Brinkman, G., R. Romain, R. Lambert and P.Stonehouse (1993), *A Review of Factors Affecting Competitiveness of the Canadian Dairy Industry,* Intercambio, Ltd., January.

11. George Morris Centre (1994), "Competition policy in the Agri-Food Industry", a report for the Bureau of Competition Policy, Guelph, Ontario, August.

12. Zwart, A.C. (1993), *Producer Controlled Marketing Organization,*proceedings of the NZ Branch of the Australian Agricultural Economics Conference, AERU Discussion Paper No. 136, Lincoln University.

13. Schroeder, B., T. Wallace and F. Mavvondo (1993), *Co-operatives, Statutory Marketing Organizations and Global Business Strategy,* Agribusiness: An International Journal, 9 (2), pp. 175-187.

14. See, for example, S.K. Martin and A.C. Zwart (1988), "Marketing Agencies and the Economics of Market Segmentation", *Australian Journal of Agricultural Economics,* 1987 and A.C. Zwart, *Controlling Exports,* proceedings of the NZ Branch of the Australian Agricultural Economics Conference, AERU Discussion Paper No. 121, Lincoln University.

15. Hussey (1992), *Agricultural Marketing Regulation – Reality versus Doctrine,* ACIL, Canberra.

16. The existence of this situation is not a problem in itself as in any competitive market, the marginal revenue is less than the product price, and thus the industry as a whole would benefit from reduced production.

17. It should nevertheless be noted that Italy imports around 1 million tonnes of milk from Germany per year.

18. Wilson, B., W.B Traill and J. Strak (1996), "The Dairy Market in the UK", a chapter in the book J. Strak and W. Morgan (eds.), *The UK Food and Drink Industry.*

19. Traill, W.B. and S. Henson (1994), "Price Transmission in the United Kingdom Yellow Fats Market in the Presence of Imperfect Competition", *Journal of Agricultural Economics,* Vol. 45, No. 1.

# MAIN SALES OUTLETS OF OECD PUBLICATIONS
# PRINCIPAUX POINTS DE VENTE DES PUBLICATIONS DE L'OCDE

**AUSTRALIA – AUSTRALIE**
D.A. Information Services
648 Whitehorse Road, P.O.B 163
Mitcham, Victoria 3132      Tel. (03) 9210.7777
Fax: (03) 9210.7788

**AUSTRIA – AUTRICHE**
Gerold & Co.
Graben 31
Wien I      Tel. (0222) 533.50.14
Fax: (0222) 512.47.31.29

**BELGIUM – BELGIQUE**
Jean De Lannoy
Avenue du Roi, Koningslaan 202
B-1060 Bruxelles      Tel. (02) 538.51.69/538.08.41
Fax: (02) 538.08.41

**CANADA**
Renouf Publishing Company Ltd.
1294 Algoma Road
Ottawa, ON K1B 3W8      Tel. (613) 741.4333
Fax: (613) 741.5439
Stores:
61 Sparks Street
Ottawa, ON K1P 5R1      Tel. (613) 238.8985
12 Adelaide Street West
Toronto, ON M5H 1L6      Tel. (416) 363.3171
Fax: (416)363.59.63

Les Éditions La Liberté Inc.
3020 Chemin Sainte-Foy
Sainte-Foy, PQ G1X 3V6      Tel. (418) 658.3763
Fax. (418) 658.3763

Federal Publications Inc.
165 University Avenue, Suite 701
Toronto, ON M5H 3B8      Tel. (416) 860.1611
Fax: (416) 860.1608

Les Publications Fédérales
1185 Université
Montréal, QC H3B 3A7      Tel. (514) 954.1633
Fax: (514) 954.1635

**CHINA – CHINE**
China National Publications Import
Export Corporation (CNPIEC)
16 Gongti E. Road, Chaoyang District
P.O. Box 88 or 50
Beijing 100704 PR      Tel. (01) 506.6688
Fax: (01) 506.3101

**CHINESE TAIPEI – TAIPEI CHINOIS**
Good Faith Worldwide Int'l. Co. Ltd.
9th Floor, No. 118, Sec. 2
Chung Hsiao E. Road
Taipei      Tel. (02) 391.7396/391.7397
Fax: (02) 394.9176

**DENMARK – DANEMARK**
Munksgaard Book and Subscription Service
35, Nørre Søgade, P.O. Box 2148
DK-1016 København K      Tel. (33) 12.85.70
Fax: (33) 12.93.87

J. H. Schultz Information A/S,
Herstedvang 12,
DK – 2620 Albertslung      Tel. 43 63 23 00
Fax: 43 63 19 69
Internet: s-info@inet.uni-c.dk

**EGYPT – ÉGYPTE**
Middle East Observer
41 Sherif Street
Cairo      Tel. 392.6919
Fax: 360-6804

**FINLAND – FINLANDE**
Akateeminen Kirjakauppa
Keskuskatu 1, P.O. Box 128
00100 Helsinki

Subscription Services/Agence d'abonnements :
P.O. Box 23
00371 Helsinki      Tel. (358 0) 121 4416
Fax: (358 0) 121.4450

**FRANCE**
OECD/OCDE
Mail Orders/Commandes par correspondance :
2, rue André-Pascal
75775 Paris Cedex 16      Tel. (33-1) 45.24.82.00
Fax: (33-1) 49.10.42.76
Telex: 640048 OCDE
Internet: Compte.PUBSINQ@oecd.org

Orders via Minitel, France only/
Commandes par Minitel, France exclusivement :
36 15 OCDE

OECD Bookshop/Librairie de l'OCDE :
33, rue Octave-Feuillet
75016 Paris      Tél. (33-1) 45.24.81.81
(33-1) 45.24.81.67

Dawson
B.P. 40
91121 Palaiseau Cedex      Tel. 69.10.47.00
Fax: 64.54.83.26

Documentation Française
29, quai Voltaire
75007 Paris      Tel. 40.15.70.00

Economica
49, rue Héricart
75015 Paris      Tel. 45.75.05.67
Fax: 40.58.15.70

Gibert Jeune (Droit-Économie)
6, place Saint-Michel
75006 Paris      Tel. 43.25.91.19

Librairie du Commerce International
10, avenue d'Iéna
75016 Paris      Tel. 40.73.34.60

Librairie Dunod
Université Paris-Dauphine
Place du Maréchal-de-Lattre-de-Tassigny
75016 Paris      Tel. 44.05.40.13

Librairie Lavoisier
11, rue Lavoisier
75008 Paris      Tel. 42.65.39.95

Librairie des Sciences Politiques
30, rue Saint-Guillaume
75007 Paris      Tel. 45.48.36.02

P.U.F.
49, boulevard Saint-Michel
75005 Paris      Tel. 43.25.83.40

Librairie de l'Université
12a, rue Nazareth
13100 Aix-en-Provence      Tel. (16) 42.26.18.08

Documentation Française
165, rue Garibaldi
69003 Lyon      Tel. (16) 78.63.32.23

Librairie Decitre
29, place Bellecour
69002 Lyon      Tel. (16) 72.40.54.54

Librairie Sauramps
Le Triangle
34967 Montpellier Cedex 2      Tel. (16) 67.58.85.15
Fax: (16) 67.58.27.36

A la Sorbonne Actual
23, rue de l'Hôtel-des-Postes

06000 Nice      Tel. (16) 93.13.77.75
Fax: (16) 93.80.75.69

**GERMANY – ALLEMAGNE**
OECD Bonn Centre
August-Bebel-Allee 6
D-53175 Bonn      Tel. (0228) 959.120
Fax: (0228) 959.12.17

**GREECE – GRÈCE**
Librairie Kauffmann
Stadiou 28
10564 Athens      Tel. (01) 32.55.321
Fax: (01) 32.30.320

**HONG-KONG**
Swindon Book Co. Ltd.
Astoria Bldg. 3F
34 Ashley Road, Tsimshatsui
Kowloon, Hong Kong      Tel. 2376.2062
Fax: 2376.0685

**HUNGARY – HONGRIE**
Euro Info Service
Margitsziget, Európa Ház
1138 Budapest      Tel. (1) 111.62.16
Fax: (1) 111.60.61

**ICELAND – ISLANDE**
Mál Mog Menning
Laugavegi 18, Pósthólf 392
121 Reykjavik      Tel. (1) 552.4240
Fax: (1) 562.3523

**INDIA – INDE**
Oxford Book and Stationery Co
Scindia House
New Delhi 110001      Tel. (11) 331.5896/5308
Fax: (11) 332.5993

17 Park Street
Calcutta 700016      Tel. 240832

**INDONESIA – INDONÉSIE**
Pdii-Lipi
P.O. Box 4298
Jakarta 12042      Tel. (21) 573.34.67
Fax: (21) 573.34.67

**IRELAND – IRLANDE**
Government Supplies Agency
Publications Section
4/5 Harcourt Road
Dublin 2      Tel. 661.31.11
Fax: 475.27.60

**ISRAEL – ISRAËL**
Praedicta
5 Shatner Street
P.O. Box 34030
Jerusalem 91430      Tel. (2) 52.84.90/1/2
Fax: (2) 52.84.93

R.O.Y. International
P.O. Box 13056
Tel Aviv 61130      Tel. (3) 546 1423
Fax: (3) 546 1442

Palestinian Authority/Middle East:
INDEX Information Services
P.O.B. 19502
Jerusalem      Tel. (2) 27.12.19
Fax: (2) 27.16.34

**ITALY – ITALIE**
Libreria Commissionaria Sansoni
Via Duca di Calabria 1/1
50125 Firenze      Tel. (055) 64.54.15
Fax: (055) 64.12.57

Via Bartolini 29
20155 Milano      Tel. (02) 36.50.83

Editrice e Libreria Herder
Piazza Montecitorio 120
00186 Roma      Tel. 679.46.28
Fax: 678.47.51

Libreria Hoepli
Via Hoepli 5
20121 Milano                         Tel. (02) 86.54.46
                                     Fax: (02) 805.28.86

Libreria Scientifica
Dott. Lucio de Biasio 'Aeiou'
Via Coronelli, 6
20146 Milano                         Tel. (02) 48.95.45.52
                                     Fax: (02) 48.95.45.48

**JAPAN – JAPON**
OECD Tokyo Centre
Landic Akasaka Building
2-3-4 Akasaka, Minato-ku
Tokyo 107                            Tel. (81.3) 3586.2016
                                     Fax: (81.3) 3584.7929

**KOREA – CORÉE**
Kyobo Book Centre Co. Ltd.
P.O. Box 1658, Kwang Hwa Moon
Seoul                                Tel. 730.78.91
                                     Fax: 735.00.30

**MALAYSIA – MALAISIE**
University of Malaya Bookshop
University of Malaya
P.O. Box 1127, Jalan Pantai Baru
59700 Kuala Lumpur
Malaysia                             Tel. 756.5000/756.5425
                                     Fax: 756.3246

**MEXICO – MEXIQUE**
OECD Mexico Centre
Edificio INFOTEC
Av. San Fernando no. 37
Col. Toriello Guerra
Tlalpan C.P. 14050
Mexico D.F.                          Tel. (525) 665 47 99
                                     Fax: (525) 606 13 07

Revistas y Periodicos Internacionales S.A. de C.V.
Florencia 57 - 1004
Mexico, D.F. 06600                   Tel. 207.81.00
                                     Fax: 208.39.79

**NETHERLANDS – PAYS-BAS**
SDU Uitgeverij Plantijnstraat
Externe Fondsen
Postbus 20014
2500 EA's-Gravenhage                 Tel. (070) 37.89.880
Voor bestellingen:                   Fax: (070) 34.75.778

**NEW ZEALAND –
NOUVELLE-ZÉLANDE**
GPLegislation Services
P.O. Box 12418
Thorndon, Wellington                 Tel. (04) 496.5655
                                     Fax: (04) 496.5698

**NORWAY – NORVÈGE**
NIC INFO A/S
Bertrand Narvesens vei 2
P.O. Box 6512 Etterstad
0606 Oslo 6                          Tel. (022) 57.33.00
                                     Fax: (022) 68.19.01

**PAKISTAN**
Mirza Book Agency
65 Shahrah Quaid-E-Azam
Lahore 54000                         Tel. (42) 735.36.01
                                     Fax: (42) 576.37.14

**PHILIPPINE – PHILIPPINES**
International Booksource Center Inc.
Rm 179/920 Cityland 10 Condo Tower 2
HV dela Costa Ext cor Valero St.
Makati Metro Manila                  Tel. (632) 817 9676
                                     Fax: (632) 817 1741

**POLAND – POLOGNE**
Ars Polona
00-950 Warszawa
Krakowskie Przedmieácie 7            Tel. (22) 264760
                                     Fax: (22) 268673

**PORTUGAL**
Livraria Portugal
Rua do Carmo 70-74
Apart. 2681
1200 Lisboa                          Tel. (01) 347.49.82/5
                                     Fax: (01) 347.02.64

**SINGAPORE – SINGAPOUR**
Gower Asia Pacific Pte Ltd.
Golden Wheel Building
41, Kallang Pudding Road, No. 04-03
Singapore 1334                       Tel. 741.5166
                                     Fax: 742.9356

**SPAIN – ESPAGNE**
Mundi-Prensa Libros S.A.
Castelló 37, Apartado 1223
Madrid 28001                         Tel. (91) 431.33.99
                                     Fax: (91) 575.39.98

Mundi-Prensa Barcelona
Consell de Cent No. 391
08009 – Barcelona                    Tel. (93) 488.34.92
                                     Fax: (93) 487.76.59

Llibreria de la Generalitat
Palau Moja
Rambla dels Estudis, 118
08002 – Barcelona
                     (Subscripcions) Tel. (93) 318.80.12
                     (Publicacions) Tel. (93) 302.67.23
                                     Fax: (93) 412.18.54

**SRI LANKA**
Centre for Policy Research
c/o Colombo Agencies Ltd.
No. 300-304, Galle Road
Colombo 3                            Tel. (1) 574240, 573551-2
                                     Fax: (1) 575394, 510711

**SWEDEN – SUÈDE**
CE Fritzes AB
S–106 47 Stockholm                   Tel. (08) 690.90.90
                                     Fax: (08) 20.50.21

Subscription Agency/Agence d'abonnements :
Wennergren-Williams Info AB
P.O. Box 1305
171 25 Solna                         Tel. (08) 705.97.50
                                     Fax: (08) 27.00.71

**SWITZERLAND – SUISSE**
Maditec S.A. (Books and Periodicals - Livres
et périodiques)
Chemin des Palettes 4
Case postale 266
1020 Renens VD 1                     Tel. (021) 635.08.65
                                     Fax: (021) 635.07.80

Librairie Payot S.A.
4, place Pépinet
CP 3212
1002 Lausanne                        Tel. (021) 320.25.11
                                     Fax: (021) 320.25.14

Librairie Unilivres
6, rue de Candolle
1205 Genève                          Tel. (022) 320.26.23
                                     Fax: (022) 329.73.18

Subscription Agency/Agence d'abonnements :
Dynapresse Marketing S.A.
38, avenue Vibert
1227 Carouge                         Tel. (022) 308.07.89
                                     Fax: (022) 308.07.99

See also – Voir aussi :
OECD Bonn Centre
August-Bebel-Allee 6
D-53175 Bonn (Germany)               Tel. (0228) 959.120
                                     Fax: (0228) 959.12.17

**THAILAND – THAÏLANDE**
Suksit Siam Co. Ltd.
113, 115 Fuang Nakhon Rd.
Opp. Wat Rajbopith
Bangkok 10200                        Tel. (662) 225.9531/2
                                     Fax: (662) 222.5188

**TRINIDAD & TOBAGO**
SSL Systematics Studies Limited
9 Watts Street
Curepe
Trinadad & Tobago, W.I.              Tel. (1809) 645.3475
                                     Fax: (1809) 662.5654

**TUNISIA – TUNISIE**
Grande Librairie Spécialisée
Fendri Ali
Avenue Haffouz Imm El-Intilaka
Bloc B 1 Sfax 3000                   Tel. (216-4) 296 855
                                     Fax: (216-4) 298.270

**TURKEY – TURQUIE**
Kültür Yayinlari Is-Türk Ltd. Sti.
Atatürk Bulvari No. 191/Kat 13
Kavaklidere/Ankara
                                     Tel. (312) 428.11.40 Ext. 2458
                                     Fax: (312) 417 24 90
Dolmabahce Cad. No. 29
Besiktas/Istanbul                    Tel. (212) 260 7188

**UNITED KINGDOM – ROYAUME-UNI**
HMSO
Gen. enquiries                       Tel. (0171) 873 0011
Postal orders only:
P.O. Box 276, London SW8 5DT
Personal Callers HMSO Bookshop
49 High Holborn, London WC1V 6HB
                                     Fax: (0171) 873 8463
Branches at: Belfast, Birmingham, Bristol,
Edinburgh, Manchester

**UNITED STATES – ÉTATS-UNIS**
OECD Washington Center
2001 L Street N.W., Suite 650
Washington, D.C. 20036-4922          Tel. (202) 785.6323
                                     Fax: (202) 785.0350
Internet: washcont@oecd.org

Subscriptions to OECD periodicals may also be placed
through main subscription agencies.

Les abonnements aux publications périodiques de
l'OCDE peuvent être souscrits auprès des principales
agences d'abonnement.

Orders and inquiries from countries where Distributors
have not yet been appointed should be sent to: OECD
Publications, 2, rue André-Pascal, 75775 Paris Cedex
16, France.

Les commandes provenant de pays où l'OCDE n'a pas
encore désigné de distributeur peuvent être adressées
aux Éditions de l'OCDE, 2, rue André-Pascal, 75775
Paris Cedex 16, France.

                                     5-1996

OECD PUBLICATIONS, 2, rue André-Pascal, 75775 PARIS CEDEX 16
PRINTED IN FRANCE
(51 96 06 1) ISBN 92-64-14911-2 – No. 48837 1996